ALSO BY LAUREN CONRAD

L.A. Candy

Sweet Little Lies
AN L.A. CANDY NOVEL

Sugar and Spice
AN L.A. CANDY NOVEL

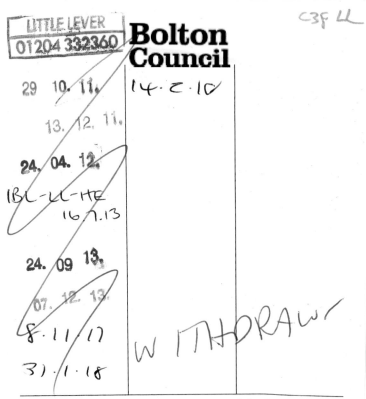
Please return/renew this item
by the last date shown.
Books may also be renewed by
phone or the Internet.

Tel: 01204 332384

www.bolton.gov.uk/libraries

25 08 18

LAUREN CONRAD
Style

LAUREN CONRAD
WITH ELISE LOEHNEN

HarperCollins*Publishers*

HarperCollins*Publishers*
77–85 Fulham Palace Road,
Hammersmith, London W6 8JB

www.harpercollins.co.uk

First published in the USA in 2010 by Harper,
an imprint of HarperCollins*Publishers*

This paperback edition published 2011

1 3 5 7 9 10 8 6 4 2

Text © 2010 Lauren Conrad
Photos © 2010 Matt Jones, Howard Huang, Kristian Dowling/Getty Images,
Angela Weiss/Getty Images and Frank Micclotta/Getty Images. Full credit and
copyright information for interior pictures appears on page 223.
Make-up chart illustrations © 2010 Kerrie Hess

Typography by Sasha Illingworth

Lauren Conrad asserts the moral right to be
identified as the author of this work

A catalogue record of this book is
available from the British Library

ISBN 978-0-00-742735-2

Printed at Butler Tanner & Dennis, Frome, Somerset, UK

MIX
Paper from
responsible sources
FSC FSC® C007454
www.fsc.org

FSC is a non-profit international organisation established to promote the
responsible management of the world's forests. Products carrying the FSC
label are independently certified to assure consumers that they come
from forests that are managed to meet the social, economic and
ecological needs of present or future generations.

Find out more about HarperCollins and the environment at
www.harpercollins.co.uk/green

This book is dedicated to the wonderful team that spends countless hours doing hair, make-up, and styling to put me together. The same team dedicated so much time and hard work to the development of this book. I am so lucky to work with such talented people and this book would not have been possible without them.

CONTENTS

INTRODUCTION ix

FASHION

CHAPTER 1: *Building Your Wardrobe* 3

CHAPTER 2: *The All-American Uniform: Jeans and T-shirts* 17

CHAPTER 3: *The Hunt: How to Shop* 37

CHAPTER 4: *Mastering Your Closet* 57

CHAPTER 5: *Accessories* 67

CHAPTER 6: *Getting Dressed: The Fun Part* 91

BEAUTY

CHAPTER 7: *Make-up* 113

CHAPTER 8: *Hair* 147

LIFESTYLE

CHAPTER 9: *Work and School* 169

CHAPTER 10: *Travel* 179

CHAPTER 11: *Events and Parties* 197

ENDNOTE 215

LETTER FROM LAUREN 219

ACKNOWLEDGEMENTS 221

CREDITS 223

INTRODUCTION

*W*hen I was six, my grandmother gave me a dress-up trunk for Christmas that overflowed with fake furs, long dresses, and costume jewellery. It sounds like a cliché but I really did swan around the house with the train of a floor-length black gown trailing behind me, a faux diamond choker, and my mother's pink satin heels. Oh, and lipstick. Every game of hide and seek required hot pink lips.

But as I've grown up, it's not games on my mind. It's meetings with my agent or a lunch date with a friend and the anticipation of traffic on Sunset Boulevard. I hate to admit this, but I'm usually running late – and while the traffic is a great scapegoat when you live in Los Angeles, it's not (always) my problem. The truth is, I'm generally late because I'm figuring out what to wear. Thankfully, I've picked up a lot of tips and shortcuts over the years, so even though I can't always get myself out of the house on time, I've got *much* better about it.

My friends blame my messy closet, but I don't think that's fair. My closet is actually a carefully organized chaos: I *prefer* to keep my clothes in a pile on the floor! I can't get out the door quickly because pulling together a look that is both adult and fun isn't easy. My seven-year-old self would throw on some jewels, heels, fluorescent cycling shorts (to, you know, make the outfit more 'daytime'), and heart-shaped sunglasses and march into those meetings looking fabulous. But that doesn't exactly fly when you want to be taken seriously.

Naturally, there's a happy medium between looking like a walking costume party and steering so far in the other (ahem, boring) direction that an outfit loses all personality.

There's a lot of noise out there, from Dos and Don'ts lists to indexes of What's Hot and What's Not. Frankly, it's nearly impossible to keep track. In my opinion, though, being a real fashion victim has nothing to do with breaking these sorts of rules: it's trying to dress like you're someone you're not.

True style and arbitrary laws do not, in fact, go hand in hand. (As far as I'm concerned, the only major fashion no-no is the kitten heel, which I strongly believe is the mullet of all shoes.) Getting dressed should be fun, because everything we wear says something about who we are – from the pattern on a shirt to the length and colour of a skirt. I filmed two reality shows, and while people had a hard time believing that our hair, noses, and story lines were real, I can guarantee that our wardrobes were. I dressed myself for the camera for five years – and never repeated an outfit once. (We filmed three to five days a week, with an average of two to three weeks off over the course of a year – that's a lot of different looks!) And as you can imagine, I really thought about what my style on camera said about my personality.

Now, I'm not saying that all my outfits were good. In fact many of them were pretty bad. But I certainly learned a few things along the way. So this book is my way of sharing a few tips about raiding the metaphorical costume trunk for inspiration and pairing it all with wear-everywhere basics. I hope it inspires you to develop your own sense of style – and to have fun with fashion.

CHAPTER ONE
Building Your Wardrobe

*T*here are a lot of opinions about what every girl should have in her wardrobe, and this usually boils down to a handful of basics. But as essential as these items may be, the thing about basics is they don't have to be basic at all. Each one should suit your personal style. Something as straightforward and simple as a blazer can be interpreted a hundred different ways. To me, it's black and tailored. To you, it might be oversized and navy. To someone else, it's shrunken and embellished. Basics – or what I like to call 'key pieces' – are the foundation around which you'll build your wardrobe; you should fall in love with them as hard as you might fall for a wear-it-once gown.

Narrowing your focus when shopping for workhorse pieces is kind of like the complicated dance of back-to-school shopping. My mom used to always try to lead me toward the things I needed (trainers, a warm jacket, nice jeans), but all I really wanted were platform sandals; midriff-baring, logo-ed tops; and bedazzled bell-bottoms. (Hey, we've all had poor judgement at one time or another.) Somehow, we managed to meet in the middle and find a happy marriage of practical and, to my thirteen-year-old mind, cooler pieces. In those moments that mattered – school dances, picture day, boy-girl birthday parties – what do you think made it out of my closet? I might not remember the names of all my crushes, but I'll never forget my happy-face-emblazoned baby tee, worn with nice jeans, of course.

I'm not dismissing how much you can come to rely on the perfect blazer or cardigan (in fact, I'm going to talk a lot about these sorts of essentials in this book) – I'm just saying that the dress that makes you feel really beautiful every time you put it on deserves a spot in your stable of can't-live-without-it pieces, too.

I think of the core of my wardrobe as the clothes that I always pack when I travel, because they're comfortable, they're flattering, and they're the items that most make me feel like myself when I'm far from home. It's a good test, actually – to go through your wardrobe and pick out your ten favourite, wear-to-death things, whether it's a white T-shirt, an argyle sweater, or a sequined miniskirt. Boiling it down will give you a pretty good picture of what your personal style is.

Now, nobody can assemble a perfect wardrobe in a day, or even a week – it's a process. I'm constantly looking at magazines and movies for inspiration, and my sense of style evolves all the time. There are always going to be mistakes, which are a part of any fashion evolution. And while I tend to play it pretty safe in public these days (I'm terrified of ending up on the Worst Dressed list), I'm test-driving all sorts of things when I know I'll be flying under the radar for a night. For example, I love crimson lips and layered costume jewellery, even if it's just with a T-shirt and jeans. Unfortunately, red lips don't always photograph well on me and a lot of jewels can look a little over the top. So while it's one of my favourite looks, it only gets its day in the sun at the local bar or a friend's dinner party. You, too, should try out an outfit when pressure is low – don't debut a new top that you're not too sure about on a first date. Wear it out with your friends first so that you know you will feel confident rather than insecure and uncomfortable.

And don't beat yourself up if you buy something that never makes it off the hanger – it happens to the best of us. But you can ensure that it doesn't happen too often if you learn what cuts and styles fit your body and your personality. I've filled the following pages with many useful strategies to help you steer clear of pieces that you may really, really want on the spot but will probably never wear. I'm all about buying what you love, but the goal here is to zero in on that foolproof, confidence-boosting wardrobe.

So let's get started.

KEY PIECES

The following items will help you establish your look. They are all versatile and can be used to build your wardrobe.

LITTLE BLACK DRESS: After nearly a century, the little black dress is still one of the greatest fashion innovations ever (thank you, Coco Chanel!). Finding a well-fitting one is essential. And thankfully, this isn't difficult, since every designer seems to offer at least one variation. Whether yours is A-line or strapless, a wrap style or a classic shape, you can wear it with tights, belted, layered with a cardigan or blazer, or just by itself and make your LBD last through the seasons. When I'm completely at a loss for what to wear, this is one of my favourite go-tos, particularly if I need to look extra-polished. Pair it with ankle boots, stilettos, or flats depending on whether you're looking to dress it up or dress it down. (See p. 98 for five ways I accessorize mine, to make it look completely new every time.)

JEANS: Denim is necessary in any wardrobe. And regardless of your body type, with all of the styles out there, you're sure to find a pair that will look great on you – don't give up in the dressing room until you've found the ones! While you aren't about to wear jeans to a black-tie event (or to prom, for that matter), you can wear them almost anywhere else. A dark wash is the most versatile: blacks and deep blues are super flattering, and they look fancier, too. (For more on jeans, see chapter 2.)

COLLARED SHIRT: Some pieces are just classics, still kicking around eras after they originally made a splash. And while they may get an update every now and then, chances are you can wear the same exact item for at least a decade. I think a collared white shirt looks great on everyone. I wear oversized versions over bikinis at the beach or by the pool, and crisp tailored styles paired with indigo jeans and high heels or tucked into A-line skirts.

SKIRT: A great skirt doesn't generally make a lot of people's must-have lists, but I think it's an essential. When you need to look a little bit fancy, a skirt is perfect. Sure, dresses accomplish the same thing (with the added convenience of being an entire outfit in one piece), but skirts are more versatile. You'll get a lot more bang for your buck wearing a skirt with flats and T-shirts for a casual look, or paired with a blouse and heels for an evening out.

BOOTS: Whether they are embellished motorcycle style, flat riding boots, or platformed knee-highs, the perfect pair is based entirely on personal preferences. And boots definitely come in handy, particularly for in-between and colder seasons. But remember, they often face the roughest weather, so don't forget to get your boots treated before taking them for a stroll.

WHITE AND BLACK TOPS: Many outfits I wear include some version of a black or white top. Whether it's cotton, jersey, silk, or chiffon, it's the perfect example of what a key piece represents: it's not necessarily the stand-out item in the outfit, but it's the glue holding the entire look together without detracting from whatever the actual centrepiece may be. I've worn white or black tops tucked into pencil skirts, draped over cutoffs, bloused over a full, printed skirt, or with simple jeans. They never fail me.

BLACK HEELS: I own a pair of sky-high black heels that look fabulous but by the end of the night I'm walking like I have a broken toe or really need to pee. So I bought a pair with a more sensible heel height. They're not spectacular – but they're comfortable and therefore practical. Eventually, I managed to find something in between – from that mystical land of comfortable and stunning footwear. They have a five-inch heel but come complete with a hidden platform, so they feel less intense. I love them so much I've had them re-soled twice.

BLAZER: A well-cut jacket is a great layering piece, plus it can pull any outfit together and make it look more polished. I love a shrunken blazer with a white tee and skinny jeans for daytime, and an oversized boyfriend blazer paired with a feminine-looking minidress at night. When you're shopping for your blazer, you can select a simple one in a classic cut or one that's got a little something special, whether it's embellishment, fun stitching, or an interesting lining.

COAT: One downside of living in sunny California is that I don't often get to reach for a winter coat, even though they're one of my favourite things to shop for. Everyone looks great in a coat. You can throw one on and walk down the street looking stylish (you could have your ducky pyjamas on underneath and nobody would know). And while a coat's main purpose is to keep you warm, you can score one that's fashionable *and* functional. Go for a bold colour or one with embellishments (half of mine sport at least one bow somewhere).

It's My Party and I'll Buy If I Want To

For my last birthday, I headed to Vegas with ten of my closest friends. I was ready for an unforgettable evening, except for one thing: I didn't have anything to wear! (I promise.) While everyone else was getting excited for our weekend of fun, I couldn't even begin to think about enjoying it until I had the perfect dress. My friends thought I was being silly. My boyfriend couldn't wrap his head around my dilemma. (I had to draw a surfing analogy for him, which is the best way to make him relate to any fashion crisis.) So two hours before I had to leave for the airport, I made a frantic trip through Saks. And then I saw it. It was beautiful. I wasn't even bothered by the fact that it weighed several kilos. (Seriously, I weighed it on my scale.) And then I looked at the price. Gasp! Out of sheer embarrassment, I won't reveal what I spent that day, but I went to Vegas and had a fabulous birthday in a fabulous dress – that I never wore again. Was it a smart purchase? Not so much. But sometimes it's okay to spend a little more than you planned if it makes you feel special.

WHERE TO SPLURGE, AND WHERE TO SAVE

Creating versatile garments that don't cost a lot of money was really important when I designed my Kohl's line. You don't always have to splurge to look good. The trick to building your wardrobe is knowing *what* to splurge on. Should you spend £350 on a trendy fringed dress that you hope to have an excuse to wear . . . someday? No! But going a little crazy on a pair of black platform sandals that you'll get a lot of use out of over time is understandable. It really comes down to a cost-per-wear situation – a £200 dress that you can wear to ten parties becomes much more affordable than a £40 dress you'll wear once and toss.

You don't need to spend a fortune on layering tops (drapey tops cut from rayon work really well – and look expensive, too) or T-shirts and jeans. There are some pieces – a hand-tailored jacket, a perfectly draped dress, a cashmere sweater, or a silk blouse – where you can see the price that you paid in the quality of the fabric and the handiwork, but if something inexpensive looks good to you, it probably looks good to everyone else.

LAUREN'S GO-TO PIECES

Key pieces look different in every girl's closet, so here's a glance at mine.

T-SHIRTS: Enough said, right? I like mine a touch slouchy and lightweight. I also like sneaking a T-shirt into a nicer outfit, like with a statement miniskirt, because it pulls the look together without stealing any of the spotlight. (For help with finding the perfect tee, see p. 33).

BLACK MINIDRESS: My black, tiered Stella McCartney dress wasn't as short on the rack; I had my tailor transform it into a mini (more on that on p. 104). I've worn it with a strand of classic pearls, paired with tights and a blazer, and under a shrunken leather jacket with gladiator heels. One dress, so many looks.

SKINNY JEANS: Black, indigo, light-washed, distressed . . . I own every variation of skinny jeans (or, as I call them, skinnies). They may not be the jean for everyone, but they're definitely my go-to cut. I wear them with a tank top and sandals, or tucked into boots with loads of layers. They are the most versatile item in my closet. My favourite pairs are from J. Brand, Urban Outfitters, and Levi's.

MAXI DRESSES: Maybe it's the Southern Californian in me, but come summer, I can often be found in a maxi dress. They're super casual but also dramatic, and if the waist hits just right (empire is the best for me), then I think they're exceptionally flattering, too.

OVERSIZED SWEATERS: Whether they're worn to the airport with leggings or layered over a sundress, I love sweaters. Because I live in California, mine are usually lightweight. I spend so many nights in strapless dresses that are so tight they literally take my breath away, all I want to do in my off-moments is slip into something comfortable. And to my mind, a beautiful sweater is equal parts glamorous and pyjama-like. Scoop-neck, V-neck, or cardigan, they all play leading roles in my closet.

BLACK HEELS: If my devotion to black platform heels isn't already clear, let me confirm it here: I own countless pairs of shoes, many of them colourful and many of them embellished, but I come back to my favourite black platform heels at least once a week. I wear them to dress up jeans or to look good (and tall) on the red carpet. Regardless of the occasion, they totally lengthen out my legs and have never let me down. (These are the ones I've had re-soled twice; I intend to keep them alive as long as possible.)

CHAPTER TWO

The All-American Uniform: Jeans and T-shirts

*I*f you can track down the perfect pair of jeans for your figure and a handful of T-shirts that fit you well, you'll have made a serious dent in building your ideal wardrobe. There's really nothing that will serve as a better foundation for putting together great outfits.

How, you may ask, do I state this with such authority? Besides the fact that I live it almost every day, the history of this all-American uniform is almost as old as America itself. (As a concept, it dates back to late-eighteenth-century France where they made a fabric called 'serge' . . . in the town of Nîmes. Serge de Nîmes. Get it? Denim . . .) It's evolved considerably over the years: at first, denim made for some pretty intense workwear (dungarees!); then in the '50s it became edgy and cool (think of James Dean's swoony outfit of choice in *Rebel Without a Cause* or, sigh, the wardrobe in *Grease*); and then ultimately, it went mainstream. Until about 1990 or so, when it reached a whole new level: designers finally decided to give it their full attention and created a gigantic market. Denim for everybody!!! There are hundreds of brands out there now, where once there were only a few popular ones (Levi's, Wrangler, and Gap).

The upside: a wealth of great options. The downside: it can be difficult to sift through all those brands and styles to find your perfect fit. But it's out there! And it is imperative that you find it. A great pair of jeans can do more for your butt and legs than any contouring bodywear – and jeans are so supremely effortless, versatile, and easy to style, that they can singularly make getting dressed a breeze.

Another timeless item, of course, is the T-shirt. As with denim, the T-shirt had a humble beginning, only to evolve into a fashionable staple (with its own iconic movie moments – picture James Dean again). What began as an undergarment – white cotton and crewneck – is now available in any imaginable colour, cut, or style. There are enough options to induce a panic attack, but through trial and error you're sure to zero in on the cut that works best for you. I like mine thin (but not transparent), loose, and long enough to hit at the very top of my thigh.

JEANS

FINDING THE RIGHT PAIR

Unless you're at a store that provides the benefit of a three-way mirror, it's crucial to bring a trusted friend with you when shopping for jeans. Finding the perfect pair is a bit like running a marathon – you'll be disappointed if you give in before you reach the end, which in this case means having the best pair in hand. This involves trying on a ton. That flattering fit is so elusive, in fact, that I buy multiples when I finally find it. Jean companies tinker with cut, fabric, and shape from season to season, so even if the style name remains the same, they likely won't be an exact match. And if you wear denim as much as I do, you know the heartbreaking tragedy of wearing out your favourite pair. So don't risk the disappointment of not being able to replace them by stocking up while you can!

Almost all denim these days has a bit of stretch built in, which is key for creating a nice line for your legs. Plus, denim with stretch is way more comfortable than old-fashioned, super-thick denim. But keep this in mind when you're trying on jeans: especially if they have 2 percent or more of stretch (check the tag inside), they should be as tight as humanly possible because the fabric will ultimately 'give' a lot. As long as they look good and you can zip and button them – and breathe! – they're not too tight. While you're in the dressing room, do some lunges and squats to stretch them out a tiny bit. If you buy them too loose, you'll have to wash them between every wear, which gets frustrating and can cause premature fading. I like to wear jeans for long periods of time between washes because I think it breaks them in a lot faster.

My legs aren't particularly long, so all jeans drag on the floor when I'm in the dressing room. Fold them under until they're the proper length (this means you need to decide whether you'll be wearing them with heels or flats) so you can get a sense of what they'll look like hemmed.

Before I drop off my jeans at the tailor for hemming (see p. 25 if you want to attempt this yourself), I turn them inside out (to protect the colour) and wash them first so that any shrinkage is accounted for. It may seem obvious, but make sure you bring the shoes you'll want to wear with your jeans to the tailor – this is a much better manoeuvre than standing on your tippy toes trying to approximate where the hem should hit. And if you don't know which shoes to pair with your jeans, turn to p. 27.

THE KEY TO POCKET PLACEMENT

The position and size of the back pockets can dramatically affect what your butt looks like in jeans – smaller pockets will make it look bigger, ones that are too close together will make it look wider. In general, choose pockets that are standard in size, which angle in slightly – they're the most flattering.

DENIM DISTRESSING

I'm generally a fan of jeans with a cleaner wash – I like pristine blues and blacks, without any machine-made whiskering or intentional, fake-looking aging. But as I wear my jeans in, I take no issue with marks from legitimate wear and

A Note About Rises …

Do you remember the time when jeans were cut with ridiculously low rises, revealing every girl in the land's underwear preference? Those days were kind of the worst. Besides requiring me to make a constant lower-back check to ensure I wasn't flashing the general public, I lived in constant fear of literally falling out of my trousers.

Because that actually happened to me.

At a school assembly.

I was wearing three-inch-rise jeans from Gap that had absolutely no stretch when I was selected during a pep rally to play a game of Extreme Twister in front of the whole school. I was already in a difficult position when . . . I attempted 'left foot yellow' and my entire butt popped out of my jeans. (Note to self: don't make enemies on the yearbook staff. . . . They have the power to include these moments in the end-of-year video. You know who you are!)

tear. They can add tons of character. And, in fact, I have a few secrets for speeding the process along.

GENTLE ABRASIONS: Costume designers have a couple methods for making clothing look old. The first is trisodium phosphate, or TSP, a powerful chemical agent that breaks down the fibre in clothing (you add it to the washing machine), but you should probably be a professional to use it (or at least practise on things that you don't care about!). If you want the effect to be subtle and strategically placed, go with the second method: use a small piece of sandpaper or a cheese grater to distress the fabric. Just make sure to concentrate on areas that make sense, wear-wise.

BLEACH: Unless you want an acid-washed pair, go gentle with bleach – you can always add more. I only use this approach on lighter-wash jeans, so the effect is a bit more understated. Dilute a tiny bit of bleach in a lot of water and dip a toothbrush (not one you intend to use in your mouth!) in the solution – then brush your thumb against the bristles, flicking the liquid onto the fabric. Once you're satisfied, wash immediately; otherwise, the bleach will continue to slowly eat away at the fabric.

MAINTAINING THE WASH OF YOUR JEANS

The downside of really richly hued jeans (i.e., pitch black or deep blue) is that the designers likely had to over-dye them to reach the shade. And while this is a great look for your legs (the darker they are, the more likely the jeans are to flatter), it can be devastating for white couches, suede bags, and T-shirts. Be careful that the dye doesn't transfer onto something you love! (I once ruined a nude-coloured Chanel bag the second time I wore it, by way of dark denim.)

Once the jeans fade a tiny bit (and are safe for all upholstery), you'll want to cling to that level of colour saturation. Be sure to always turn your jeans inside out when you wash them (otherwise you run the risk that the colour will be stripped in weird swathes), and if at all possible, hang them to dry (they won't shrink as much with this approach, either).

Rit Dye has special formulations for black denim, which are great if you need to liven up your jeans; Dylon's classic denim wash is excellent, too.

HOLE REPAIR 101

Small holes in the knees aren't a big deal, but if your jeans start to give out in the crotch area, that can be a deal-breaker. Fortunately, there are companies like Denimtherapy.com that will re-weave rips – using thread that's an exact match. They charge by the inch, which is significantly cheaper than it would cost you to buy a new pair. (Plus, worn-in jeans are kind of irreplaceable, right?) If the knees start to give out completely, consider transforming them into cutoffs. Don't snip too much at once – start conservatively and roll them until you're satisfied with the length. You can always make them shorter but if you Daisy Duke them right off the bat, you'll never be able to make them respectable again.

HOW TO HEM YOUR OWN JEANS
(IF YOU'RE IN A HURRY)

If your legs are as short as mine, you probably need to hem every pair of jeans, too. Which means you've definitely experienced those times after you buy a new pair when you want to wear them immediately – not right after the tailor is finished with them but *right this very second*. It's actually not that difficult to hem them yourself and to keep the original stitching intact. Depending on how well you sew, it could be a permanent solution, though I usually have my tailor redo them once I'm ready to part with them for a few days. A temporary fix isn't a bad thing to do, either, if you can't decide whether to turn them into 'flats' or 'heels' jeans – you may as well test-drive a length first.

- You have to put the jeans on to figure out exactly where you want the hem to hit. Use a tape measure to get the desired length. Take the number of inches you need to lose and divide by two.

- Take the jeans off and, with one fold, cuff them. The length of that fold should be one half of the number of inches you need to lose.

- Stitch around the fold directly below the original hem – you want to be as close to this line as possible.

- Flip the fold so it's on the inside of the leg and iron them down. There should be an invisible hem at the bottom of the jean, so it looks like there's no break in the fabric.

PERFECT JEAN AND SHOE PAIRINGS

It's not rocket science, but different jean styles beg for different types of shoes – the right choice can completely change the line of the leg. These are by no means hard and fast rules, just suggestions!

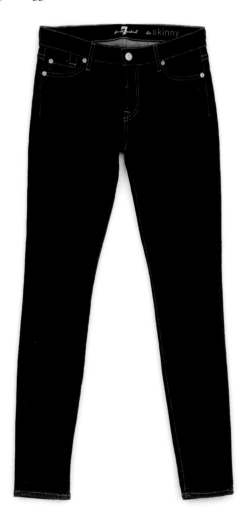

SKINNY JEANS: This will always be my jean cut of choice, but I know that the proportion gives lots of people heart palpitations – make sure that there isn't excess fabric gathered at the ankle (have your tailor remove it) so that it's a nice clean line, from the thigh to the foot. Otherwise they can make you look dumpy.

SHOE CHOICES: I usually wear mine with heels, just because those extra inches really help lengthen out the leg, but they work great with simple flats, too. This is also the ideal jean for pairing with high boots since you're not dealing with lots of excess, bulky fabric.

STRAIGHT-LEG JEANS: Probably the most universally flattering cut, the straight-leg styles are great because they're clean and sophisticated. If you're looking for a work jean, this is a good bet, particularly if you go for something in a basic blue or black. A distressed pair is perfect for the weekend. If you love the look of a skinny but aren't brave enough to try one, a straight leg is a good compromise.

SHOE CHOICES: Much like with skinnies, a flat or heel is always a good choice. Because a straight leg isn't wide enough to fall over your shoe like a boot-cut jean, have them cropped to the ankle – in fact, it's actually a really flattering trick and will make your legs look *longer*.

TROUSER-STYLE JEANS: This is another popular work option because they tend to be slightly higher in the rise and have a proper trouser-style closure (i.e., a tab rather than just a button). I like tucking a shirt into these and layering a thin cardigan over. I try to avoid anything too high in the waist – wear them if you're inclined, but I have yet to see a girl I think they truly flatter.

SHOE CHOICES: Because the trouser leg will cover the shoe, you can go for a wide range of options (including heels that are a little beaten up). If you want to wear your jeans with trainers (like a Jack Purcell Converse or a Ked), this is a good style to choose since the material will conceal them. Plus, the dressed-up nature of the jeans counters the casualness of the shoe.

BOOT-CUT JEANS: These were pretty revolutionary when they hit the scene because they're flattering on almost any body shape. This is primarily because the slight flare at the bottom balances out any curviness in the hips. Make sure that they're the perfect length, though. If there's a puddle of material on the floor, they have the opposite-of-flattering effect and will just make you look big.

SHOE CHOICES: So-named because of their versatility with boots, these are good with any sort of heel, booted or otherwise. Definitely skip boots that need to go *over* the jeans, though, since your calf area will be swimming in material.

BOYFRIEND JEANS: The super-baggy jean is one of those trends that re-emerges every few years – and for good reason. They're unbelievably comfortable and can also be quite flattering, so long as you balance out the proportion. I know they're essentially the sweats of the denim world, but you have to pair them with a fitted or tailored top so that you don't look sloppy.

SHOE CHOICES: I normally wear a thin sandal or simple ballet flat with this style. Because this cut is super casual and baggy, you might need a heel to make it a bit fancier – plus, the extra height will help you pull off all that fabric.

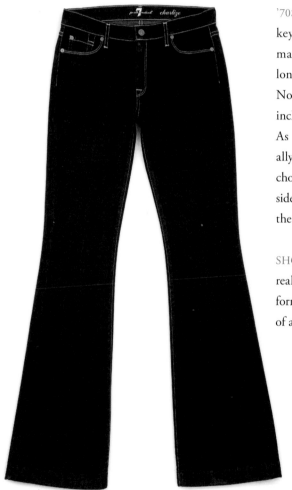

'70S-INSPIRED FLARE JEANS: The key to this particular trend is to make sure that you leave them super long and find the shoes to match. Normally I like to leave about an inch between jeans and the ground. As a general rule, these should literally skim the earth. This is a great choice if your legs are on the shorter side, since all that fabric will create the illusion of longer legs.

SHOE CHOICES: Anything with a really, really high heel, from a platform to an ankle boot. I love the idea of an earthy, woven wedge.

T-SHIRTS

HOW SHEER IS TOO SHEER?

T-shirts are so simple in concept, but they can be a total disaster in execution. I love that designers are paying so much attention to them: there are now hundreds of options, many of which feature loads of innovations fabric-wise, but all of this choice can make it a bit more difficult to whittle the field down. And just as denim makers took the 'low-rise' craze a little too far a few years ago, T-shirt manufacturers have gone a little crazy in their quest for the perfect paper-thin material.

Many of the T-shirts out there these days are just too sheer to flatter. A quick field-test while shopping for T-shirts is to stretch the fabric over your hand – if your palm is visible underneath, then all those parts you might want to conceal on your stomach or sides will be visible, too. Granted, this doesn't mean that you need the super-thick versions of yesteryear, but the T-shirt should have some opacity, and maybe a tiny bit of structure. You want it to glide over your curves, not cling. When you find the perfect T-shirt – soft, long, slouchy, concealing – buy multiples!

FLATTERING SLEEVE LENGTHS

It's funny how dramatically sleeve length can affect the look of a T-shirt. (If you don't believe me, roll your shirtsleeves while looking in a mirror.) You want the sleeve to hit at either a thin point of your arm or at a point where your muscle has peaked and is starting to dwindle. If the sleeve stops at a point on your arm where the muscle is extending out, it will make it look much bigger than it actually is.

HOW TO LAYER T-SHIRTS

If you accidently bought some aforementioned overly sheer tees, hold on to them for layering purposes. I love a sheer T-shirt under a strapless dress (it makes them totally appropriate for day). You could also wear one under a second, equally sheer shirt. The bottom layer should be slightly longer than the top layer.

HOW TO KEEP WHITES WHITE

There's some sort of chemical reaction between sweat, deodorant and cotton that creates those unsightly yellow stains. You can attack the problem with a few different approaches (but skip the bleach since it doesn't help at all here). One trick is to soak the stained area in hydrogen peroxide (you can dilute it in water), another is to pop an aspirin or two into the washing machine (wait until it's full of water), or you could soak the offending T-shirt in a solution of vinegar and water (1 tablespoon of vinegar to 1 cup of water).

CHAPTER THREE

The Hunt: How to Shop

*L*ike you would on any day spent in the wilderness, you should have a good plan when preparing to shop. It's important to know not only what you are hunting but the best places to look – and the proper attire and appropriate ammunition are key, too. Whether you're narrowing in on the coolest crocodile clutch or a killer pair of Gucci heels, a lack of planning might just leave you empty-handed or worse, totally dissatisfied. So lace up your boots, polish your credit cards, and get ready for the hunt.

Make it easier on yourself by wearing comfortable shoes – a good day of shopping involves a lot of legwork. If the weather is nice, wear a skirt or dress. (Taking jeans on and off is tiring . . . and don't get me started on tights!) I usually add a tank top layer into the mix, too, because even though boutiques hate it, if there's a line for the dressing room, you can just slip blouses and sweaters on in the middle of the store.

I prefer to shop alone so that my decision-making process doesn't get muddled by someone else's personal style. For example, my best friend and I have very different taste. Whenever we shop together we toss a lot of loving barbs, like 'Yeah, that's cute . . . if you want to look like a circus runaway.' In the past, I've let myself be influenced by other people's opinions, but these days, I really don't want to be talked out of buying something I love just because it's not to someone else's taste. That said, the right set of trusted eyes can be handy. A good shopping partner should be honest but kind – with a working knowledge of your closet. That is, someone who can steer you away from those items you already have a ton of, whether it is jeans or turquoise party tops. And someone who can clue you in to the fact that something isn't flattering without destroying your self-esteem.

It's key to figure out how much you're willing to spend before you set foot in any stores. This budget should define what you think the demands of your shopping list require (shopping for basic tees would mean a smaller budget, a new winter coat would mean a bigger one), and the outer limit of what you can afford. If you tend to get carried away with credit cards, bring cash instead. It's much harder to hand over £20 notes than it is to keep swiping plastic. And it will make you think very carefully before you commit to any purchases, which is good news for your wallet *and* your closet. (You don't want to overload your wardrobe with impulse buys that make it difficult to see the pieces you actually wear all the time.)

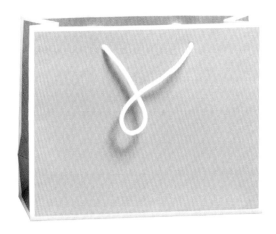

TACKLING DEPARTMENT STORES AND MASS CHAINS

As a wise woman once said, always do a quick lap before committing to a location. (Yes, I just quoted Cher from *Clueless*.) She was talking about a party, but I think this also applies to a large department store. I usually cruise around the main floor before circling back and grabbing the pieces that caught my eye the first time around. You should go with your immediate instinct, because if an item jumps out at you from the racks, it will also jump out at you in your own closet. If you shop as often as I do (Hey now! I have to keep up on trends for a variety of projects – it's rough, but someone's got to do it . . .), quick, instinctual shopping is a good way to stop yourself from buying too much. When I'm on the prowl for understated basics, I take the time to flip through the racks. This is particularly important if said key piece is black or navy – it can be really hard to see the detailing within a mass of other similarly hued pieces.

Skipping Regret

Although the dreaded 'why did I buy that?' experience is all too common, at one point or another we all experience the 'why *didn't* I buy it?' blues, too. That dress that fit perfectly but was slightly too expensive. The shoes that you thought were too trendy, only to be trolling eBay looking for them two seasons later since you can't get them out of your mind. I've come up with a system to minimize these regrets: most stores don't have a problem holding items for a few hours, so when I find myself doing the 'do I really need this?' dance, I simply put the garment on hold for the day and continue shopping. If I still want it a few hours later, I swing by and pick it up. If I've forgotten about it or feel even a tiny bit of relief at the money saved, then I don't bother.

DRESSING ROOM STRATEGY

I don't know if it's the stale, over-circulated air back there, but dressing rooms tend to be soul crushing and energy draining. (Small space + scary lighting = my version of a tiny hell.) So enter prepared! Bring multiple sizes so you don't have to head out for more, and try things on in the appropriate order (don't leave yourself topless, for example) if you're planning to leave the fitting room for an impromptu fashion show for your friends.

If you tend to lose steam halfway through the trying-on process, tackle the most intensive pieces first (dresses, jeans) and save the easy-peasy ones for last (cardigans, blazers, coats). Also, prioritize your favourites: if you find something on the racks you sort of like but aren't sure about, bring it with you. If you can't muster the energy to try it on after you've worked your way through everything else, you'll have answered the question of whether you need it after all.

It's important to sit down in any trousers/jeans/skirts/dresses you're trying on because you'll want to know if they're comfortable if you need to sit for an extended period, and if trousers ride too low in the back or skirts and dresses rise too high. It's also a good idea to leave the dressing room area to both get an idea of how a garment moves on you and see it from another perspective or in different lighting: unless I have a friend with me, I always make sure to check myself out in front of at least two mirrors (some are likely skinny, others won't be so generous). There's nothing worse than getting home and trying on a purchase, only to find out that you were conned into thinking it was flattering!

AVOIDING IMPULSE PURCHASES AT HUGE, WALLET-FRIENDLY STORES

The one thing I strongly believe should not cost a fortune are layering tops, so I can often be found in that section of H&M or Forever 21, stocking up on tanks and shirts made from synthetic fabrics like rayon or modal. They tend to be really swingy, and the fact that they don't cling is super flattering. If you're buying key pieces like that, forge ahead, regret-free.

Sometimes, though, a little restraint would've helped me out. I'm sure I'm not alone here, but I've wandered into a big chain store – whether it's American Apparel, H&M, or Topshop – only to wander out hundreds of dollars poorer. I'm still not sure exactly how it happens. One minute I'm admiring a pretty £20 top and the next thing I know I'm standing at the cash register with a pile of clothing two feet tall. Now, mathematics wasn't my strongest subject (please hold the obvious joke here), but the logic seems rather elementary. Lots of small numbers equal a big number, and yet I'm always standing at the register scratching my head . . . £300?!?! And while I've found some great things in these accidental sprees that I've worn to death, I've also managed to fill my closet with many 'did-I-really-need-this?' items. I don't usually make these irrational choices when the clothes are more expensive – only when they are so affordable that there's seemingly no choice to be made. Danger! Don't buy something just because the price is right.

TREND TESTING

Before you commit to a scary or expensive trend, you can test-drive it with a budget-friendly option. For example, before splashing out for a leather bomber jacket, try a faux leather version that costs £50 first. If you decide you love it, chances are the real deal that's going to last for years and years is a sound investment.

REAL   DEAL

HITTING BOUTIQUES

Unlike a department store, a boutique doesn't have the benefit of thousands of square feet to appeal to every kind of shopper. While this can mean fewer options, it also means less to search through, which is a decidedly good thing. Each boutique tends to have a specific style, and so this means that you need to shop around for the right boutique for you. There are lots of benefits to localizing your shopping. For one, once you're really familiar with a store's staff and merchandise, you'll know that you have a place to turn to for any fashion emergency. And secondly, you're much more likely to stumble upon little-known designers, which means a closet full of more original pieces.

SECRET WEAPON: SALESPEOPLE

I tend to be a pretty quiet and low-key shopper, i.e., a pushy salesperson can drive me nuts. But a *knowledgeable* salesperson can be a great resource. The best ones tend to know everything on the racks, which means they can draw your attention to items you might have otherwise overlooked – and expedite the entire process by bringing you things to try in the dressing room and letting you know if pieces run big or small. If you are a loyal customer you can

Return Policies

It may sound like a no-brainer, but make sure you check the return policy – I usually assume that boutiques will be lenient. Some are, and some really are not. A full refund within thirty days of the purchase date is pretty standard, though some will only give store credit. This is not ideal but workable if it's a boutique that you frequent.

Meanwhile, if you make a big purchase at a department store, keep an eye out for mailers. Often, if a sale starts soon after you've just bought something, they'll honour the discounted price if you bring the piece back in with the receipt.

Go for Custom

There are many items in my closet that I love so much, I wish I could wear them on a weekly basis. This is usually due to the fact that they fit really well and are therefore both flattering and comfortable. So I've started taking my favourites to a tailor to have him re-create them in a bunch of different fabrics (same dress, different print!). It's not necessarily a cheap undertaking – though definitely worth pricing out, particularly if you'd like multiples of the same thing. (They only have to draft one pattern, which is the time-consuming part.) When you go to the fabric store, make sure you have the original garment on hand so that they can help you source the correct quantity of a similar-weight material – if the original dress is denim, it might be more difficult to have it reproduced in silk, for example.

reap the benefits of a salesperson watching out for you. Once they become familiar with your preferences and tastes, they can call you to let you know when something arrives that you might like (and sometimes even hold your size if you say pretty please) – and most importantly, they'll clue you in when the pieces you're eyeing hit the sales rack. I also always ask how anything statement-making is selling – if they've had to re-order it several times, I don't buy it, since I can be assured I'll see other girls wearing it all over town.

TACKLING
VINTAGE

One advantage to wearing vintage is that you're probably never going to see the same thing on someone else. For any of you who have shown up to school, prom, or a wedding wearing the same dress or top as someone else (I shared a limo to senior prom with two other girls in the exact same dress as me), you can understand how valuable a one-of-a-kind can be. It's special. But finding the perfect piece can also be a lot of work. There are tons of higher-end vintage stores that do the heavy lifting for you – they search high and low for fabulous clothing and accessories that they then clean and display nicely. This sort of shopping experience generally comes with a pretty steep price tag, though.

If you have the time, patience, and inclination to roll up your sleeves and do the thrifting yourself, a Saturday spent digging through piles of old clothes – whether it's at a flea market or the local charity shop – can yield some amazing steals. I once found a beautiful vintage Dior nightgown that I wear as a blouse for only £5 – it's one of the loveliest things in my closet, and probably one of the cheapest!

THE FINE LINE BETWEEN COSTUME AND LEGITIMATE OUTFIT

If you become a devout vintage shopper, you're definitely going to encounter a lot of clothes that you absolutely love, but just can't figure out how to update enough to wear. Sometimes, I buy these things anyway: you never know when styling inspiration may strike, plus it's nice to own and look at beautiful things. And sometimes you need a costume. Case in point, I fell for a beautiful, pristine white flapper dress with crystal-dusted straps that I had to have. I've only worn it once – to a Halloween party – but I love to look at the craftsmanship behind it every once in a while.

DEAL-BREAKERS

If a vintage garment is stained, chances are that stain is never going to come out (most likely it's been around for as long as the article of clothing has) – some blemishes, though, are easy to work around. If it's near the bottom of the hem, you can always shorten the dress. Or it might be in a place where it's possible to conceal it with a belt, brooch, or scarf. Extreme discolouration – yellowing under the armpits, for example – is another flaw that's pretty much non-negotiable. (And kinda gross . . . pass!)

There's a lot of debate about whether you can get smells out of vintage clothing because there's really no point in looking fabulous if you're going to be stinky. Fabrics like polyester

– which were extremely popular in the '60s and '70s – tend to retain, if not create, body odour, which means that they're not good candidates if they smell less than lovely. A musty mothball odour, though, can generally be eradicated with some Febreze, or a gentle turn in the dryer with multiple sheets of a fragrant fabric-softening sheet. You can also seal the clothes in a plastic bin with a few scent-soaked cotton balls for a few days. (Make sure the balls don't touch the fabric.)

JUDGING QUALITY ON THE FLY

Though I believe that the quality of the piece doesn't always matter – if you love it, buy it! – there are a few tricks for determining how much care went into producing the garment. Fine fabrics – silk, thickly woven cottons, chiffon – speak for them-selves. Flip over the hems and check the work. Hand-stitched items definitely get extra points (and can give you an idea as to their age). The tag is also a major clue as to when the garment was made – woven tags generally indicate a higher production value than anything printed or mass-produced.

RESISTING LABELS

I'm a sucker for name brands, but just because something is Chanel or YSL does not necessarily mean you should buy it – unless, of course, it's amazing! (Or really, really cheap.) I am sure that Emilio Pucci velvet trousersuit was fabulous in the '70s, but are you really going to wear it to your next cocktail party? Sometimes you have to resist an amazing thing, too – like if it's not your size. When you see that perfect dress or blazer lurking on the shelf, make sure it fits or is an easy alteration (some things, like the width of the shoulders on a jacket, are completely non-negotiable), otherwise that piece will live in your closet, gently mocking you, forever.

UPDATE IT!

Don't be afraid to take scissors to something that has great components but just doesn't work as a whole. I bought a beautiful dress made from a gorgeous fabric with ruffles – but the shape of it was really outdated. So I took out some sheers and a sewing kit, cut the sleeves off that sucker, and hemmed the top. Ta-dah! I was left with an updated strapless minidress.

In the same vein, consider cutting a sequined butterfly top down the front to turn it into a jacket or wearing a fancy button-front shirt as a coat. Sometimes dresses even work better back to front, particularly if the front neckline is really high-cut. Get creative!

SHOPPING ONLINE

I always feel like a cliché when I do it, but shopping in my pyjamas never gets old. (I shop for pyjamas in my pyjamas!) Not only does it make me feel slightly more productive when I'm watching TV (multitasking!), but it gives me access to designers from across the globe. Also, clothes often look much more appealing on an actual model rather than hanging on a rack, so I feel like I stumble on things that wouldn't have otherwise caught my eye. Lastly, while stores only offer a limited range of pieces in certain styles and colour, online retailers tend to have a larger selection.

Of course, when you purchase things without trying them on, there's a chance that they're not going to fit. This is when it becomes extremely important to check a site's return policy – along with shipping rates. (Occasionally you'll even encounter a frustrating 'restocking' fee.) Smarter websites make the whole process incredibly easy (and offer lots of incentives like free shipping), so avoid those that make it too hard.

EDUCATE YOURSELF IN THE FIELD

For the greatest success rate, limit purchases to lines you're already familiar with fit-wise. This is especially important when purchasing trousers and jeans. If you don't know where to begin, the next time you're in a huge department store or at a boutique with a large denim wall, take the time to try on as many different brands as you can.

It's also a good idea to write down the style number of an item you're coveting but might not feel ready to buy (or can't find in your size). A quick Google search can yield a range of prices – who knows, it may be discounted at another shop. If the style number doesn't return any results, search by brand and description.

USE THE FIT MODELS

It helps to pay attention to how pieces look on the fit models. In fact, some sites, like Revolveclothing. com, even provide their measurements and list the size they're wearing. This is great because you can do a quick size comparison from brand to brand. (She might be a 27 waist in one make but a 28 in another, for example.) Also, if you're looking at a screen full of denim shots – all modelled on the same girl – you can get a pretty good idea of which are going to be the most flattering, even if your body in no way resembles hers. (When something looks less than ideal on a fit model, chances are that it's tough to wear.)

SWIMWEAR SHOPPING

Remember how I said that coats are one of my favourite things to shop for? Well, guess what my least favourite thing to shop for is. . . . Here's the thing about buying swimwear: you should really do it in the comfort of your own home. If, for some reason, you want to feel bad about yourself, go ahead and try one on in a store dressing room. Between the fluorescent lighting and the unflattering mirror angles, you'll never want to set foot on a beach again. Instead, order swimsuits online at the end of the summer – when your skin is still a little sun-kissed and you're in decent shape – and try them on

*The First Places
I Look Online*

For key pieces: Shopbop.com
For jeans: Urbanoutfitters.com
For special pieces: Netaporter.com
For trendier pieces: Topshop.com

*Best Online
Sample Sale Sites*

Get on the mailing list of these online sample sites (items sell out almost immediately) – different designers go on sale on different days.

Gilt.com
Giltfuse.com
Ruelala.com
Hautelook.com
Editorscloset.com

in your bedroom. You'll get a much more realistic idea of how the suit looks, plus you can jump around a bit and make sure that it holds you in and moves with your body. (Picking at bikini bottoms is not the look of the summer.) If a suit doesn't fit right, send it back and try again. (Always check the return policy, as some sites are strict about swimwear.) Also, learn what brands fit your body. A lot of companies change their prints and colours from season to season but will keep a few signature styles. If you find one you love then you can just re-order new suits and trust that they'll fit perfectly.

One thing I like to do is mix and match swimsuits. Sometimes a loud print on a two-piece can be a little much, but just wearing the bottoms with a solid top looks great. (Or alternately, stripes and polka dots are adorable together.) Also, it's tough to find really flattering bottoms, so if you stumble upon some, buy multiples and then mix in new tops. Two bikinis, one solid and one print, becomes four. That's the kind of multiplication I can appreciate.

SHOPPING EBAY: HOW TO KNOW IF IT WILL FIT

Most sellers on eBay will list measurements along with the garment's hangtag size. This comes in handy if you're looking at vintage pieces, since sizing has changed dramatically over the past few decades. Next time you're at the tailor, ask him or her to write down your measurements. (This is better than doing it yourself, since it can be difficult to figure out where your true waist is, for example.) The jewellery and accessories on eBay are the real treasure trove, because no measurements are required! That said, read the description closely – it's impossible to tell scale from a photo, and the seller is required to list any defects or flaws. Remember, you can always take jewellery to your local jeweller to be cleaned or have small repairs made. (Repairing a broken clasp or re-sizing a ring are easy fixes.)

FINDING THE DEALS

There are a ton of websites that aggregate coupon codes and shipping promos all in one place – Shopittome.com, Luxgoddess.com, Luckymag.com – so you can be sure that you're getting the best possible deal. It's also wise to follow your favourite brands on Facebook or Twitter, since they alert their fans to pre-sale events and special discounts online. The same goes with email lists at small, independent boutiques.

CHAPTER FOUR
Mastering Your Closet

*T*he last time I seriously overhauled my closet it took a crew of four people (including a professional organizer and a stylist), three full days without sunlight, and countless food deliveries. I wouldn't call myself a pack rat – or worse, a hoarder – but I do have a habit of hanging on to things. Dropping beyond-repair shoes down a trash chute or sending my T-shirts off to Oxfam seems so final. So these items had slowly accumulated behind my closed closet doors. But with all that stuff in there, it became harder to find *any* clothes in my closet. And if you can't see it, you won't wear it. By the time of the intervention, it had got so bad that I started shopping for new clothes because I was afraid to dig through my closet for something to wear. Knowing that this was not a one-man job, I enlisted reinforcements. I needed to be held accountable. For example, my stylist (and good friend from high school) and I really battled it out over a pair of pink, crystal-studded heels from my college formal. He argued that 'sentimentality' did not justify a spot in the closet. So heartless, particularly because *he* was my date to that formal! But I'm grateful for everything they did and said because in the end we were able to create a beautiful, easy-to-shop closet. The hangers are matching and equally spaced; the clothes are organized by category, style, colour, and sleeve length. And I even found a tiny little spot in a bottom drawer for my pink, crystal heels.

Though I vowed to keep the chaos in check, I've found that I need to re-evaluate the contents of my closet every six months or so. By that point, it's bad enough to consume an afternoon (not a long weekend), but the underlying closet-organizing principles haven't been completely destroyed. I can pretty much eyeball what is supposed to go where.

Granted, I would love to be more disciplined about it. In fact, I even tried to institute a rule that I'm not allowed to buy something unless I give something else away. But if you remember from the introduction, I don't follow rules when it comes to fashion! (I do think it's a good idea, though, and if you can stick with it, you'll be one step ahead of me.)

There are lots of ways to make the closet-organizing process less painful and more fun. The enjoyment factor is essential, since the key to an easy-to-shop closet is in doing the physical work and trying on every single thing in there. And as anyone who has to brave multiple pairs of potentially ill-fitting jeans in one sitting can attest, friends and food go a long way in making it a little more palatable. (Remember that scene from *Sex and the City* when Carrie cleans out her closet with her friends?)

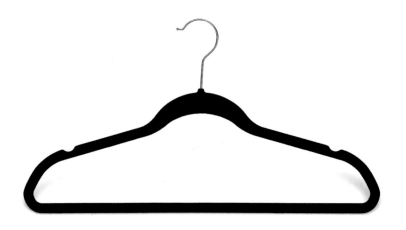

EDITING YOUR CLOSET

The first order of business is to tidy up the room that houses your wardrobe as much as possible, because it's about to get realllly messy. Make sure that your friend(s) have a comfortable place to sit. You'll need them to stay high-energy to cheer you on.

Take out every single thing in your closet and move it all to a corner of the room. Make sure you have a clear work space for a large holdall, two canvas totes, and some trash bags.

TRY EVERY SINGLE THING ON:

a. If you try on anything that's ripped or stained beyond repair, it goes in the trash bag.

b. If you try on something and you're over it at first glance, place it in a second, separate trash bag, which will go to a charity, like Oxfam or the Salvation Army.

c. If you try on something that's ill-fitting but cool, put it in a tote bag, which is destined for a visit to the tailor's.

d. If you try on something and it's not great on you but would be perfect on a friend, place it in the second tote bag.

e. If you try on something and realize you haven't worn it in at least a year but don't feel quite ready to part with it, place it in the holdall.

f. If you try on something that's a clear winner, it's earned a spot back in the closet.

Everything that's staying should be put back facing the same direction. Ideally, the hangers should be matching. I like Huggable Hangers, because they save space and they're flocked, which means pieces won't slip off and fall on the floor. Buy them in bulk and save some cash (for more clothes!).

When you put the chosen pieces back in the closet, group like with like: all dresses in one section; long-sleeve shirts, another; short skirts, another, and so on.

Most importantly, prioritize the hanging space according to what you wear the most. If it's work shirts, those should be in the most accessible and visible place. Things that you don't need that often – like black-tie dresses – should live in the back corners.

After everything you've decided to keep is hanging, go back and arrange each section by colour. This is useful not only because it helps you see where each category begins and ends (making it simple to put the day's outfit back where it belongs), but it also gives you a good sense of where you might be overbuying: if you have a huge collection of red tops, keep this in mind when you're shopping. (The one circumstance where this is sometimes not true is with black: if you wear a lot of black, and you hang all those pieces together, it can be impossible to tell them apart. Sometimes it's good to intersperse a few white or grey items in there, too, just to break it up a bit.)

After you've tackled the closet, move on to your chest of drawers. The same process applies (though rejected lingerie and socks should not go to the Salvation Army – those go straight in the trash).

BREAKING UP WITH YOUR CLOTHING

Remember that holdall packed with clothes that you don't hate but haven't worn lately (see option 'e')? It's time to dispense with it. Some people are really good at tossing things without over-thinking it. I am not one of those people. It takes me about six months to convince myself that I can live without something that I forgot I even owned. But there are a few steps for easing the process and getting the clutter out of your life.

I've learned from experience that taking a bag of discards immediately to the Salvation Army just induces panic. So instead, I pack the bag and leave it under my bed. After six months have elapsed, I peek inside. Very rarely, I will rediscover an article of clothing that I'd actively been missing, but more often than not, I can't believe that I even bothered to hold on to it for that extra length of time, and I cannot wait to donate it all.

ORGANIZE A CLOTHING SWAP

Looking for something to do on a Friday night? Make some snacks and invite your friends over for a clothing swap party. The idea is to shop your friends' wardrobe cast-offs without exchanging any money (just clothes). It's not necessarily always going to be a one-for-one situation, but the beauty of it is that you can set the swap terms as you go. (It might also be necessary to take turns, since it can get a little frenzied if people begin competing for pieces.)

CASH IT IN:
CONSIGNMENT STORES VS. EBAY

A lot of people have managed to make a considerable amount of money selling closet rejects. The easiest way is to take your higher-quality clothes and accessories to a local consignment store. (They generally take a cut of whatever they manage to sell the item for.) If there aren't any places like this in your town, you can do it through a service online (Covetshop.com or Yoogiscloset.com, for example). If you have the patience, you can make a bundle on eBay, too; you just have to be diligent about taking really good pictures and offering a detailed description of the piece, including measurements.

THINGS THAT CAN BE REPAIRED

A good tailor can completely remake a piece of clothing so long as it fits in a few key places like the shoulders (see p. 104 for more on this). If you're trying to decide whether to keep or toss an item, consider whether it might not work better shorter, tighter, or looser. Like that pesky collection of ugly bridesmaid dresses or that winter formal dress from two years ago: some might work well as cocktail dresses. These are things a tailor can fix for you.

If moths attack your favourite sweater, clean it first to limit future damage, and then take it to a re-weaver, who will seamlessly patch all the holes using the same colour and texture of fibre.

If you wear out your jeans, send them off to a company like Denimtherapy.com. They re-weave denim according to the wash of the jeans – and charge by the inch.

HOW TO FOLD, HANG, AND STORE PIECES SO THAT THEY LAST LONGER

IN A HANGING CLOSET: Take everything out of dry-cleaning bags immediately (the plastic traps harmful chemicals, which will eat away at fabrics) and rehang all of your clothes on either tubular or flocked hangers. Anything heavy, like a sweater dress, should be folded so that it doesn't get stretched out in the shoulders. Also, most dry cleaners will recycle hangers. Returning them guarantees they won't collect in your closet – plus, it's a nice way to be green.

ON A SHELF: When you're creating stacks of folded items, put the bulkiest pieces at the bottom – otherwise you'll end up with teetering piles. You can bury cedar balls or chips in between your sweaters to stave off moths – and be sure to keep them all as clean as possible. Moths are attracted to body odour in natural fibres. Icky, but true.

IN A DRAWER: Due to the lack of visibility, I try to use my dressers only for things that are better left unseen: socks, underwear, swimwear, plain T-shirts, tanks, and workout clothing.

Displaying Your Clothes

Your clothes don't have to be confined to your closet. I keep my favourite shoes lined up on a long dresser along one wall and have a rolling rack of garments all in a similar colour scheme displayed in the corner of my room. Beautiful clothes are meant to be seen, so why not show them off?

HOW TO HAND WASH CLOTHING

It's kind of a pain, but if you can muster the energy, hand wash all your delicate tops and cashmere sweaters. Besides being really bad for the environment, dry cleaning is hard on clothing, so use it sparingly.

I like Woolite, since it smells great, though there are companies like The Laundress that create cashmere-specific detergents. Fill a clean sink or bucket with warm water and soap, and get to work: it doesn't have to be an overly laborious process. I soak a sweater for a few minutes and then work the suds into the fabric, wringing it out as I go. Once the water runs clear, gently squeeze as much water out of the material as possible and then place it flat on a dry towel, which will help the sweater maintain its original shape. Roll the towel and press gently down.

And speaking of the dry cleaner . . .

If you're not the sort of person who has the time to do hand washing or drop clothing at the cleaner's, don't invest in clothing that needs special care. Read tags carefully before you get to the cash register, otherwise you'll end up with a mountain of too-dirty-to-wear items and ultimately, an outrageous cleaning bill.

CHAPTER FIVE

Accessories

*I*f you took a poll, I think you'd find that accessories of all types are any girl's favourite thing to shop for: besides being beautiful objects, there's no pre-dressing-room anxiety about whether they're going to fit and you don't have to strip down to try them on. Plus, one simple accessories switch-up can completely change an outfit. If a jeans, T-shirt, high-heel combo seems too boring, swap in a pair of red ankle boots or a statement necklace for a completely different look. And the next day, those same accessories can transform tights and a basic cotton dress into something edgy and cool. If you're bundled up for winter but want to feel a little less . . . wintry, reach for a brightly patterned scarf.

Even though accessories are a prime candidate for an impulse purchase, resist. You should put just as much care into building your accessories collections as you do into building your wardrobe.

And remember, the right accessories can also save you money, because you can use them to update pieces you own, instead of buying all new clothes. So, let's say you spend a season in bubble dresses. When the trend goes away the dress doesn't have to – just belt it to achieve an entirely different silhouette and therefore a whole new look.

SHOES

Of course, there's more to a good shoe collection than stilettos. Even if you favour a particular style, it's nice to have some variety in your footwear. Your feet work hard for you so the least you can do is buy pretty things to put on them.

THE BASICS OF SHOE SHOPPING

You can't go wrong with a beautiful pair of court shoes, right? (They don't even take up valuable hanging space!) Wrong. There are some serious considerations to keep in mind before setting foot into the shoe department.

Walking in a shoe department has pretty much no correlation to what it feels like to actually walk down the street. Have you ever noticed that they're always carpeted? This is because a five-inch stiletto is way more comfortable on plush pile than hard asphalt. Make sure you take the shoes for a spin on hardwood floor (or whatever hard surface is available) before you buy them.

Leather – and particularly suede – stretches. But it's not going to stretch in length, only in width, so if your toes are crammed into the end, they're always going to be crammed into the end. And if they're swimming from side to side, that problem is probably only going to get worse. The general rule is to shoe shop at the end of the day, when your feet are swollen, to get the most realistic idea of what's going to work. Keep in mind that there are minor tweaks to create a more bespoke fit (for more on this, see p. 75) – but you're never going to change the size remarkably.

A CLASSIC SHOE WARDROBE

The categories here are pretty general – the specifics are totally up to you. But if you hit all the notes below, you'll be covered for all of life's main events.

FLAT: From plain ballerina styles to something patent and colourful, nothing beats this category for comfort. It's nice to own at least one pair that's special, too, so look for something embellished or that has a stone-studded front.

COURT: You should have at least one black pair, though it doesn't have to be overly conservative – go for something classic. Then get one in a fun colour, too.

PEEP-TOE: These are sexy because they're subtly revealing. Look for them in a pretty, feminine colour, like a soft grey or mauve.

EMBELLISHED: Think of this pair as the perfect counterpoint to a simple black dress, so consider jewels or sequins, or a fun, bright colour.

GLADIATOR: These are a fun option because they're a tougher version of a sandal. But be sure to pay close attention when you try them on because they can be uncomfortable around your ankles.

BOOTS: Whether you prefer heeled or flat, pick a classic, straightforward boot, something you love now but could also see yourself loving two years from now. A good pair of boots can be costly, so just be sure to spend wisely.

DOUBLE THE LIFE
OF YOUR SHOES

I know it's totally heartbreaking, but if you buy a pair of shoes that you'd like to keep for a long time, you absolutely have to take them to a cobbler first. (Okay, admission: I can't help myself and usually wear them once before doing this.) Spend the extra £10 or so to have a rubber sole added – they'll last twice as long.

TROUBLESOME ANKLES

Having shorter legs means that any sort of shoe that cuts me off at the ankle is tough. (Jealous, right?) This includes everything from ankle boots to gladiator sandals to T-strap heels. If it's approaching the problematic area, the trick is to find something that dips slightly in front, whether by design or because it's a little loose and drapey. Definitely avoid a strap or swath of leather that creates a straight line, which will completely cut you off. If I fall in love with a pair that doesn't do my legs any favours, I purchase the shoes in black and wear them with black tights to create a longer line.

Tricks of the Trade: What Your Cobbler Can Do for You

It can be a difficult process, but shop around for a great cobbler. (Ask your favourite department store or shoe boutique who they use in the area.) I can't tell you how many times I've been told that something can't be fixed (a snapped heel, for example), only to find a pro who makes the injured shoe look brand-new. Besides basic repairs like retapping heels or adding rubber soles, a good cobbler should be able to stretch too-tight-in-the-calf boots or add special insoles to make a pair that's too big fit. (There are drugstore solutions for this, too, though they don't work quite as well.) I've also had my shoe guy re-dye ballet flats that have seen better days into a slate grey or black. This is particularly key if you have a pet who has fine taste in shoes: my dog Chloe loves to chew off heels, and I've been lucky enough to find a cobbler who can bring them back to life.

BAGS

There are the bags we love, and the bags we actually use – and then there are those that can be both. Keep in mind that bags are dreamed up by artists, not architects, which means that style *always* trumps function in the design process. While you want a tote that's beautiful, it should be practical, too. If you stick to a fairly conservative dress code, a richly hued bag is a great way to make your outfit a little more exciting.

SHOPPING FOR BAGS 101

First things first, assess how much the bag weighs when empty. If you're anything like me, you schlep around significantly more than a day's essentials, which can get heavy! So make sure that you're starting with a piece of leather that doesn't already weigh several kilos. And beware of lots of extraneous hardware – I love the look, too, but it can make a straightforward bag totally unmanageable. (Making your boyfriend carry it for you is not a good solution!) While still at the store, take out all the paper stuffing, and put the contents of your own bag in there. Does it all fit? Does the bag hang well?

While you're at it, make sure you're considering all those minor – but important – details of your life. Do you need to carry a computer? (Pick something with sturdy handles.) Do you walk a lot? (A cross-body satchel is a good solution for hauling a lot of weight over a long period of time, plus it allows you to keep your hands free.) Do you leave pens uncapped? (Go for something black or navy, which will conceal stains.)

TRICKY MATERIALS – HANDLING SUEDE AND PATENT LEATHER

Suede is always a super-soft choice, but one of its downsides is that it can pick up colour transfers from almost anything (beware of those over-dyed jeans, for example). It can also get a little nubby when it wears out. You can fix this by brushing over the affected area with a nail file. Patent leather tends to be pretty sturdy, though it can pick up stains – easy to remove via a cotton swab doused in nail polish remover.

A BAG FOR EVERY OCCASION

Bags come in different shapes and sizes. You should own an everyday bag that works with your lifestyle, but you can't wear your everyday bag *every* day, so it's good to have options for when a bag swap is required.

EVERYDAY BAG: Choose one that's comfortable to carry, fits all your things, *and* looks stylish.

CLUTCH: For nights when I want to travel light, I love a clutch. It's small, classic, and feminine. It's generally worn with something special so I opt for one in a neutral colour — that way it doesn't steal the spotlight.

EVENING: I'm always careful not to go too tiny when it comes to an evening bag: I will never be that girl who can survive for a night with a credit card, ID, and a handful of twenties. It has to be large enough to contain all my essentials, plus lip gloss, a camera, and my phone.

OVERSIZED CLUTCH: Previously relegated to evening hours only, an oversized clutch is one of my main daytime go-tos: its smaller size requires an edit, which means I'm not hauling around lots of unnecessary things . . . like five magazines.

LARGE: A large bag should be spacious enough to contain everything you need during the day without the threat of stretching out the leather or snapping the strap.

TRAVEL: The best travel bags can accommodate a change of clothes, a good book, and a computer – not too precious but chic enough to work as a day bag once I arrive at my destination.

JEWELLERY

With enough willpower, you could compile a pretty comprehensive clothing and accessory wardrobe in a short amount of time. But that's not always the case when it comes to jewellery. It's nice when shoes and clothes have sentimental value (you know, the dress you wore on an amazing first date or the 'lucky' shoes you're convinced landed you your first job), but most just don't. With the jewellery that you wear every day, though – which admittedly has absolutely no utilitarian function – there's probably some underlying story that makes it special.

I have a huge cache of costume jewellery that I dip into all the time, but for the most part, it's not the stuff I wear on a daily basis. Those slots are reserved for the pieces that matter, which are best accumulated over time. Jewellery is different for everyone, so some people treasure their big diamond studs, simple silver bangle, or delicate gold chain strung with charms that took years to collect. I'm always reaching for a familiar ring or necklace when I'm nervous or far from home. It might sound cheesy, but it's nice to have tokens nearby from people you care about. Of course, you can't always count on all your jewellery to be gifts; sometimes you want to buy a little something for yourself – and that's nice, too.

LAYERING JEWELLERY 101

When it comes to jewellery, my first instinct is the more the merrier. That said, if I'm making a big statement around my neck, I'll downplay my earrings – or wear no earrings at all. There's something about an oversized earring/necklace combo that seems dated – plus, they tend to compete. In the same vein, if I've added an armful of bracelets, I skip rings on that hand. Really, it depends if you are wearing a statement piece or if you want a little bit of everything. If your necklace, bangles, and rings are a little more dainty and don't fight with one another then don't be afraid to put everything on together.

EARRINGS

Of all types of jewellery, these are the most important things to try on before you buy. A pair that looks delicate on a friend might completely dominate your face, depending on the shape and size of your head. I suggest investing in one small everyday pair of earrings, whether they are little diamond studs or small gold hoops, and a handful of larger pieces for special occasions.

NECKLACES

Layering necklaces shouldn't be a complex undertaking. It should really just be a happy jumble around your neck. Granted, if you get more than four necklaces going, they'll probably get tangled. You can avoid this by layering necklaces that are of different lengths, from super long, almost navel-grazing chains to something that hits right at the clavicle. I keep some spare chains around at the three main lengths – 12", 14", and 18" – so that if I need to swap out some pendants, I can.

BRACELETS

This is a great opportunity to mix more precious and delicate pieces with tougher, bolder pieces. A few simple gold bangles, some chains, and even a friendship bracelet all look great together. I love layering an eclectic mix of jewels on my arm.

FAKE IT UNTIL YOU MAKE IT: CHEAP JEWELLERY

When it comes to fun, on-trend jewellery, you don't have to spend a fortune: Topshop, Alltherageonline. com, and your local jewellery wholesale district are all great resources. (Despite the implications of the latter, they normally all sell to the public.)

And when it comes to full-on diamonds, you don't need gigantic, bling-y studs, either. There are tons of great alternatives. Don't get fixated on karat count and instead go for a piece of jewellery that feels like you.

DIAMOND CHIPS: A lot of jewellers use flat, diamond chips to create the same effect – for a fraction of the price.

PASTE: Readily available on eBay and in antique stores and flea markets, paste jewellery began to crop up in the 1800s. It's leaded glass, backed on foil, and painted to look like the real thing. You can find extremely intricate and gorgeous pieces, which still cost almost nothing compared to the real thing.

CUBIC ZIRCONIA: If you want some straightforward studs, CZ is a good alternative. Don't go crazy on the size – the more moderate they are, the more realistic they'll appear. (These are nice if you're constantly losing an earring like me.)

Keeping Jewellery Organized

There have been some sad times in my life when my necklaces have become so tangled that I haven't worn them in months – it can take hours to separate a pile! Fortunately, I've stumbled upon a few fail-safe ways for keeping them organized. (And see p. 184 for tips on travelling tangle-free.)

JEWELLERY TREE: You can find these at stores like Pottery Barn and Urban Outfitters. Essentially, they're designed to look like an Eiffel Tower or spindly tree or some other structure that has lots of little arms. Give each necklace its own branch or prong, just to ensure that they don't mingle.

PINS: Go to the craft store and pick up some long pushpins with pearlized ends and stick them into the wall. (This doesn't have to be perfect.) They're strong enough to hold up delicate chains, and they create a really pretty pattern on the wall.

BEDPOSTS: Use your jewellery as a display – I drape necklaces over doorknobs and bedposts in my bedroom.

GLOVES

I think a lot of us associate little ladylike leather driving gloves with our grandmothers, but this so shouldn't be the case! I love a brightly coloured pair with a black, brown, or white jacket. If you're walking around on a chilly day, nobody gets to see the outfit under your coat, so this is your best way to show off your sense of style (and keep your fingers nice and toasty).

SCARVES

There's been a gigantic scarf resurgence in the last few years – and for good reason. They're one of the easiest ways to add a dose of colour, texture, and pattern to an outfit – like a statement necklace but comfortable and warm! One of the best things about them is that they don't cost a fortune, unless you're springing for a fancy silk version or oversized cashmere wrap. I tend to stockpile the long, thin ones since they're the easiest to wear. Reserve louder prints for simpler outfits, whereas neutral-hued options work with almost anything.

ALTERNATIVE USES FOR SILK SCARVES

It can get frustrating to keep a silk scarf around your neck (it's slippery!), so I like to fold mine into a thin strip and tie it onto the handles of a neutral bag. It's an elegant way to add a touch of colour and pattern. You can do a knot, or a bow – don't be too precious about it!

Sometimes I use one as a hair accessory. Choose a relatively narrow scarf for this (if there's too much material it gets a little bulky): fold it until it's about three inches wide, and then place it in your hair as you would a headband. Tie it underneath your hair, and voilà! A chic spin on the bandanna!

THE UNEXPECTED ACCESSORY: NAIL POLISH!

I know it seems like it shouldn't quite qualify (it is a beauty product, after all), but I think of nail polish as an outfit finisher. When I'm wearing clothing that's neutral and understated, I often opt for something a little out there on my nails, whether it's a near-black red, metallic purple, or even a neon pink. It's a great way to play with colour without committing in a bigger way, and it's a fun way to test-drive a trend (yes, there are even trends when it comes to nail polish) without feeling like you're wearing it all over your body. It's easy to take off, it flatters every skin tone, and it's cheap! What could be better?

CHAPTER SIX

Getting Dressed: The Fun Part

*W*hen you're on a reality TV show 'playing' yourself, it's important to figure out what your personal style is – and quickly. It's even more important to figure out what's flattering! As I mentioned earlier, there was nobody to help me. During my five years on TV, I never used a stylist for filming: it was entirely my responsibility to make sure that I didn't repeat an outfit. That doesn't mean I never wore the same thing twice, though. My favourite skinny jeans, high-waisted skirts, and loose white tees made countless appearances – I just had to make them look completely new. For this, I developed a few useful tricks.

The first was to look for ideas everywhere – editorial spreads, street-style blogs, the girls brunching alongside me on Saturday mornings – and to take quick notes or tear out pages of looks from magazines that I wanted to try at home. It's a good strategy for finding inspiration, and for stealing ingenious styling tricks (like pinning a handful of vintage badges to an otherwise straightforward blazer or putting together a completely monochromatic outfit). Plus, gathering a ton of different images will help you get a good sense of what it is that you like. (You might find that every single thing you respond to visually is preppy, or Victorian, or some combination of the two.)

The second trick was to grab a fashionable friend and a digital camera and start styling and snapping. When you're feeling inspired, you'd be amazed at how many different looks you can wring out of just a handful of pieces over the course of an afternoon. (If you're stumped, read on – I've done a lot of the legwork for you in the following pages.) If you figure out fifteen outfits, you have fifteen remedies for those days when you feel like you have nothing to wear (and they happen . . . way too often!). Now, if I were a different person and much, *much* more organized, I would have created a continuity binder, which is what costume designers and wardrobe assistants rely on when they're shooting a movie. (Scenes are never shot in order and they need to keep close track of when an actress wears each outfit so the various scenes slot together seamlessly.) Oh, how I wish I had documented what I wore on *The Hills* – it would have been the best reference guide to my closet, ever. But that said, it doesn't have to be complicated: perfect an outfit, take a picture or jot down some notes, and you're good to go!

And finally, I learned to stop thinking about a garment on the rack as an almost sacred, untouchable thing. Sure, some things are just right the way they were made. But that's the rare exception. For the most part, everything needs a tiny bit of customization, whether it's as simple as rolling the sleeves on a shirt, or as extreme as cutting a vintage dress in two and just wearing the skirt. Point is, getting dressed shouldn't be about perfection; it should be liberating and fun, in the same way that digging into your dress-up trunk when you were a little girl was the best way to spend an afternoon. To be honest, I still have a dress-up trunk, and not only for Halloween. I'm always adding a silk scarf here or a vintage hairpin there. I've collected costume jewellery for years and have more than I can wear (see p. 81 for more on this).

So, if you have a big event – an interview, a party, a first date – don't wait to figure out your outfit until the last minute. This just leads to panic attacks. Start thinking about it days in advance so you can luxuriate in the process – getting dressed is really the best part!

FOOLPROOF OUTFITS

Here's a handy cheat sheet to some of my go-to Date and Weekend looks. (For work and school outfits, see chapter 9, and for party suggestions see chapter 11.)

DATE NIGHT

First dates are one of the most fun – and most stressful – occasions to dress for: what you choose to wear says a lot about you, so it's important to figure out exactly what message you want to send.

A lot of people say that you should look good while simultaneously looking like you didn't try. I'm all for low-key elegance, but I think that making a visible effort is the right move. When you think about it, isn't it sort of rude not to? This doesn't mean that you need a formal gown and a full face of make-up (I sometimes wear lipstick on a first date, though – it discourages the guy from going in for a kiss, which is convenient since I try to stand by the no-kissing-on-the-first-date rule), but it does mean that it's a good thing if they can tell that you dressed nicely for them.

My end goal is to look like a more polished version of myself.

I always ask for a general idea of what we will be doing so that I can pick the right clothing. I learned this rule after I was walking out the door to meet my date when he texted me to tell me to bring socks. It took me a second to decode this: he was taking me bowling. I was wearing a mini-dress and heels – so not the best choice! It's also kind of key to find out how tall he is so that you don't inadvertently tower over him (unless, of course, that's your thing).

The other X factor of date dressing revolves around the amount of skin to expose. Guys generally want to see your body, but that doesn't mean that they need to see the whole thing. Pick one part that you want to show off – whether it's your shoulders or your legs – and keep it demure elsewhere. You want to feel sexy – but comfortable. And I don't care what sort of justification you offer, but anything too tight or too short isn't sexy *or* comfortable!

Ultimately, I'm not above getting a guy's opinion. Girls view fashion in a very different way, which is why we love high-waisted trousers and conceptual tops. Your friends might sign off on an outfit that would make an average guy scratch his head.

DAYTIME DATE

Even if your date is during the day you should still look nice. Just because you're meeting for coffee or a stroll in the park instead of dinner doesn't give you licence to slack. If it's a sunny day and you're feeling girly, wear a flirty dress or skirt. Nice jeans and a pretty top will work if you want to keep it casual, but no trainers with this option, please. Instead pair it with pretty flats, boots, or heels.

WEEKEND

The weekends are one of the few times in life when you should feel liberated to wear whatever you want. But, if you're anything like me, you might find that it's challenging to look relaxed without slipping into sloppy territory.

There is a big grey area between a put-together outfit . . . and sweatpants. I know it can be difficult after a long week of enduring cinched waists and uncomfortable heels, but fight the urge. Sweats were made to be worn inside your home, not to the supermarket, airport, or on late-night frozen-yogurt runs. You can be comfortable and look great; it just requires a little more effort. So stock up on easy pieces that don't take much thought (tanks, sundresses, casual T-shirts).

Small upgrades make a huge difference: simple things like swapping your boring flip-flops for an embellished pair can instantly make an outfit more interesting. The weekends are also a great time to try a trend that you've been eyeing but don't feel comfortable wearing to work or school.

ONE LITTLE BLACK DRESS, FIVE WAYS

Here's an example of how one dress can be worn many ways – and how much accessories can influence your look.

BOHEMIAN: Vintage jean jacket, lace slip, sandals

EVENING: Embellished stilettos, great clutch, nice jewellery

PREPPY: Cardigan, pearls, Mary Jane heels

CASUAL: Oversized cardigan, ballet flats

EDGY: Leather jacket, gladiator ankle boots

STRATEGY GUIDE

MIXING PATTERNS

Whether it's stripes and checks, or florals, paisleys and polka dots, wearing two patterns at once can be surprisingly chic. There are a few things to keep in mind.

- Choose patterns that share a neutral background, like brown, black, white, or grey.

- Make sure that the patterns have at least a few colours in common: if you're mixing a navy stripe shirt with a floral print skirt, make sure that a similar blue is part of the floral print – this is important if the two items don't share the same neutral background (see the first point).

- Mix up the scale of the prints: a teeny-tiny polka dot with big, oversized stripes – or even stripes on stripes, so long as they're not the same size.

- Don't go overboard: only two pieces in one outfit should have a pattern, and there should be at least one other element (a cardigan, tights, belt, or skirt) that's completely plain.

MIXING VINTAGE AND NEW

I love working vintage clothes and accessories into my wardrobe (see p. 47 for more on sourcing the good stuff), but it has to be kept in check. Try to limit yourself to one vintage piece per outfit (like the vintage shirt I pair with my black skirt), otherwise you run the risk of looking too era-specific, or like you basically raided your grandma's closet. This is even more true if you're wearing a major vintage piece like an evening gown or a day dress: if this is the case, skip the sequined cardigan or the fur stole. Instead, update the ensemble with an on-trend item like a cropped leather bomber, an oversized boyfriend blazer, or ankle boots. It's all about mixing it up: surprising combinations tend to look fabulous and can make an otherwise dated garment look fresh.

For those of you who freak out at the idea of wearing someone else's discarded clothing, think about mixing in a few vintage accessories instead, whether it's a bejewelled necklace or a woven leather belt. (Full disclosure: I'm a little iffy on vintage shoes – it just seems kind of yucky.) It really is one of the best ways to add patina and texture to an outfit. And, if you're willing to hunt, buying vintage often costs a fraction of what you'll pay for a comparable item that's new.

HOW TO FIGURE OUT
THE PERFECT STYLE PROPORTION

The most important rule is to dress for balance. If you're wearing skinny jeans or something equally fitted below, pair them with a more voluminous top. Alternately, if you're working a drapey blouse, skip the baggy boyfriend jeans. Nobody looks good when their body is drowning in fabric, but an overly body-conscious, tight-all-over look isn't very flattering, either. (Leave a little to the imagination, ladies.)

When I'm getting dressed, I think about the part of my body that I'd most like to play up that day. If it's my legs, I put on my skinnies (they're kind of a uniform, to be honest) – and then usually add some variation of a slouchy tee or an oversized blazer. If I'm wearing a short dress, I make sure it's not too tight. (Again, showing a lot of leg is revealing enough.) But if I want to wear my volume on the bottom – full skirt, boyfriend jeans – then I make sure that I'm pairing it with a fitted tank or jacket. Really, it's a balancing act.

If there's a specific body issue that you're trying to dress around – whether it's an overly endowed chest or a boyish figure – turn to p. 111 where I address it all.

WHAT A TAILOR CAN DO FOR YOU

There's a misconception that everything we buy should fit flawlessly – but beyond the fact that nobody really has the body of a true fit model (the figure around which all the patterns are constructed), most of us aren't perfectly proportioned, either. (I'm definitely not – for more on this, see p. 109.) And the true irony is that at any photo shoot – whether it's for a magazine or a catalogue – if you were to turn the fit model around and shoot her from the back, you'd see about fifty safety pins and thirty binder clips all over the item of clothing being modelled. This is the quickest and easiest on-site way to make something look tailor-made during a photo shoot without enlisting an actual tailor. (For more on what happens at photo shoots, see p. 213.)

There, I said it: a tailor. Sure, it's not necessarily cheap, but having someone customize your clothing for you is the fastest way to a bespoke fit. You can't exactly walk around with a back full of binder clips! Having someone take in and let out your clothing wherever necessary will do much more for flattering your figure than a hundred consecutive days at the gym.

HOW TO MAKE
THINGS FIT PERFECTLY,
ON THE FLY

If a garment doesn't need significant alterations, there are lots of minor tweaks you can make in seconds.

HEMMING: A light, quick, running stitch along the bottom of a dress or skirt that needs to be shortened is actually easy: no fashion degree or sewing machine required. Basic thread leaves no mark behind if you need to pull it out and start over – or if you ultimately decide to replace your handiwork with the real deal. (For tips on shortening your own jeans while preserving the original hem, turn to p. 25.) I also keep a bin of safety pins on hand, since sometimes you just need two or three of those to make short work of a simple hem (particularly if it's on a part of the garment that's not very visible). Alternately, double-sided hemming tape from a company like Bristols 6 accomplishes the same thing: I usually iron the crease first to give it extra staying power.

CUFFING: It's one of the simplest styling tricks out there, but a quick cuff – on a jacket, shirt, or trouser leg – is an easy way to make a piece look a little edgier. It's also a great way to rein in extra volume (just roll the fabric under a bit before you cuff it) if something is swimming on you (like a men's collared shirt). It doesn't need to be perfect or symmetrical. Often, I push my sleeves up my arms a bit after cuffing them, just to make it look a little more laid-back and undone.

BELTING: There is generally no better ally for a girl than a great belt, since the waist is invariably always good to highlight – nothing accomplishes this more effectively than a waist-cinching wrap. And in this age of the voluminous top, it's the best means for tackling all that extra fabric, too, which generally drowns a lot of girls' figures. A belt is also very handy for making a skirt that's a little too big work – I fold the waistband over a tiny bit, pin it, and then use the belt to conceal my handiwork.

PINNING: If a top is too big and you don't feel like using a belt to create a waistline, pull a handful of fabric together in the back, and pin it with a vintage brooch. It takes about a second but is super chic. Just make sure that you're not going to need to sit all night because it can be a little uncomfortable to recline on jewellery.

HOW TO WEAR COLOUR

It's a bummer that so many people are colour shy, because it's one of the most appealing ways to make an outfit more interesting. Black is chic and all, but red is wayyyy more fun. If you're a bit reluctant, start with small doses (a shoe or a bag) and work yourself up to a brightly hued top. For the truly adventurous, consider layering variations of the same shade: like a mint-green top under a forest-green cardigan.

Sadly, there's no universal colour chart that will tell you exactly what shades are most flattering for your skin tone. In fact, it changes all the time, from season to season. (There are lots of colours I can pull off when tanned that I would never attempt in the dead of winter.) The quickest way to tell if something will work is to hold it up to your face under a fairly bright light to see what it does to your complexion. If there's no mirror handy, the general rule of thumb is that the deeper and more jewel-like the tone, the more wearable it becomes. Anything pastel or washed out can get dicey – fast.

And if your favourite colour turns you pasty (for me, it's purple – which I love, despite the fact that it makes me look terrible), that doesn't mean that you can't wear it at all. Just don't wear it next to your face. Instead, opt for a skirt, trousers, or even shoes in variations of that tone.

STYLE IS LAWLESS

Not to belabour the point and all, but it can't be said enough: there are no rules when it comes to fashion. You can wear white all winter (ivory-hued trousers look great with riding boots and a big, oversized sweater), despite those old-fashioned types who say it should all be stashed after September. It's difficult to do, but black and navy can happily co-exist in the same outfit. (You just need to mix up the textures – a navy blazer doesn't work that well with black work trousers but definitely integrates nicely with black jeans.) Look around for good style inspiration, and you can make almost anything work.

BODY ISSUES

When you live in a city like Los Angeles, you're bound to encounter a ton of body dysmorphia: in fact, I have yet to meet a girl – starlets and models included – who is completely happy with her figure. This is pretty tragic, when you think about it, and a colossal waste of emotional energy. Listen: I will never love my thighs – it doesn't matter how much my weight may fluctuate, but my upper legs stay the same. (To me, they're short and wide.) But you've probably never singled out my thighs as overly well endowed, right? This could be because I'm the only one who notices. Think about this when you're turning the microscope on yourself. You can pick anything apart, which is why I always think it's the best policy to overlook those parts of your body that you don't love, in favour of playing up the parts of your body that you do. So I try to ignore my upper thighs, and show off my shoulders and collarbone instead.

THE FLATTERING POINTS
ON ANY WOMAN'S BODY

This may sound a little crazy but stick with me here: there are a handful of points on every woman's figure that are almost universally delicate and feminine: the wrists, the ankles, and the collarbone. Making them visible, whether it's via a bracelet-sleeve jacket, a pair of cropped jeans, or a V-neck top, is always flattering.

HOW TO SHOW OFF YOUR . . .

SHOULDERS AND ARMS: Strapless dresses instantly draw the eye to the upper arm and shoulder area. And any sort of halterlike top accomplishes the same thing. (If you're narrow up top, this will make you look a bit broader across the back.) I usually purchase tops one size larger so they drape off my shoulders and look more feminine.

LEGS: When it comes to skirt length, there's really no standard for a flattering cut. Some girls love their knees and like to reveal them – others would rather cover them with fabric. Just take your skirt and use your hands to lift and lower the hem to see what looks best. Also if you prefer a higher hemline but don't want to show too much skin, tights are always a great option.

Keep in mind that the fuller the skirt, the thinner your legs will appear – anything too tight will have the opposite affect. (The worst is the sausage-in-casing look.)

And you don't have to show a lot of skin to play up your legs: a pair of well-fitting skinny or straight-leg jeans accomplishes the same thing.

CLEAVAGE: There are a lot of things you can do to play up your cleavage without busting out a deeply plunging top and a push-up bra. Subtlety is really important here since anything overly revealing gives off a slightly trashy vibe. I think a good guideline is to never show more than three-quarters of an inch of shadow, which you can accomplish via a scoop-neck or V-neck T-shirt or sweater. Tip: if your top is loose *and* low-cut, make sure you're not flashing everyone when you bend over.

BUTT: Anything fitted through the butt and hips is a good choice, whether it's a knee-length pencil skirt or a great pair of black trousers. The key is to make sure that you don't wear anything too volume-heavy, such as an A-line skirt or a pair of overly baggy trousers, otherwise you'll just look large rather than curvy.

WAIST: Don't disguise your waist with a lot of fabric (such as a tentlike top). Instead, go for pieces that are tailored, like a collared shirt, or a T-shirt that's not too slouchy. As mentioned, a waist-cinching belt is a great way to draw attention to an hour-glass shape (or to create one from scratch). If you're wearing multiple layers, including a jacket, go for one that either nips in or is cut off right at the waist. Both are a great means for drawing the eye to this part of the body.

HOW TO DOWNPLAY YOUR . . .

UPPER ARMS: Steer clear of cap sleeves, which are a tough length to pull off unless this area is slim and toned. Instead go with either a three-quarter-length sleeve or a blouse that has a bit more volume in the sleeve (which makes the arm look thinner in comparison). A batwing top is also a great fix; they can change the entire silhouette, distracting from the problematic area.

THIGHS: As mentioned, this is my least favourite part of my body. I love an A-line skirt because they don't cling to the thighs. Also, because my legs aren't particularly long, I shorten most of my skirts and all of my minidresses an inch to create the illusion of length.

Normally, a skinny jean would be terrifying for a girl with thighs, but I counter mine with longer shirts (to keep that troublesome upper leg area covered) and I make sure that extra fabric doesn't pool around my ankles; that's a common problem with skinny jeans. It destroys the line of the jeans, which tends to be unflattering. For a girl with thighs, a boot-cut jean is a no-brainer, too – a slight flare below really balances out the proportion.

TUMMY: Stay away from clingy revealing fabrics; choose a thicker, more structured material instead. This will help create a sleek line while concealing any extra bumps or lumps. Patterns tend to make people look bigger, so choose solid colours up top.

I always love an empire-waisted top, too. It's one of my favourite choices for a night out that's going to involve a lot of eating. You definitely don't have to worry about sucking your stomach in, particularly if the shirt is cut from a jersey or heavy cotton!

If you want to wear a more curve-hugging piece, then scoop up some Spanx. They'll minimize rolls and smooth out your figure. The heavy-duty ones are a little terrifying and make it somewhat difficult to breathe, but once in a while you've literally just got to suck it up.

CHEST: If you're well endowed, the worst thing you can do for your figure is to choose a blouse that shoots off your chest (i.e., a tent). This will instantly add about ten pounds to your shape. In the same vein, shy away from shirts that have extra material along the top – whether it's through ruffles or draping. You don't want any additional volume there at all. Go for streamlined, sleek, and tailored.

HIPS: Hips are hard to conceal since they're part of your skeletal structure – but they're also very sexy! If you think you're too curvy below, consider ways to balance out your figure by adding some width up top – highlighting your waist the entire time. If you've got a '50s pinup-girl shape, play it up!

CREATING THE ILLUSION OF A PERFECTLY PROPORTIONED BODY

Here's the thing: the goal here is to reflect the idea of a perfect body, not actually possess it! Most people would argue that an hourglass shape (of varying degrees, according to personal preference) is the general ideal, particularly if you have any curves at all. So it really comes down to the balance: if you're a bit bottom-heavy, counter it by adding some volume up top. If you're top-heavy, the reverse is true. Structured clothing can transform your entire shape. That said, everyone has a different idea of the perfect body. So if you've got it, flaunt it (in a classy way).

CHAPTER SEVEN
Make-up

I started wearing make-up when I was thirteen. I had one of those crazy palettes with about seventy-two different eye shadow colours, which was pretty convenient since, back then, I liked to match my eyelids to my outfit. I used (and wore) an excessive amount of purple, a colour that doesn't actually do me any favours; maybe this is why I don't wear eye shadow anymore! The kit also came with two 'face' colours, with which I did a fair amount of experimenting. One was for skin much darker than mine, the other for skin much lighter. I tried the lighter shade, and it made me so pale that on one of our family Christmas cards I looked like a mime. Whenever I do anything awful, my mom threatens to post that picture on the internet.

Like everyone else I know, I basically taught myself how to do make-up – and created a lot of cringe-worthy photo moments in the process. You're bound to make a lot of mistakes, but that's an important part of the learning curve. With time and help (like from this chapter!), you'll figure out your own way to play up your best features, without looking like you have too much of a 'face' on.

In addition to learning by trial and error, I've been lucky enough to work with a lot of talented make-up artists over the years, and have picked up tons of tips. (FYI, don't be shy about asking for tutorials at your local make-up counter – especially if you're willing to buy a product or two.) Amy Nadine Rosenberg is one of my all-time favourite make-up artists, and she helped me develop what I now think of as my signature look. I love Amy not only because of how she wields her make-up brushes but because she's always respectful of my comfort level. Like with eye shadow: however irrational my fear of it might be (I think it makes me look older and overly made-up), she never puts it on my face. We've all been coached to believe that every make-up component is essential for a 'complete' look, but that's just not true. Read on, because Amy provides tons of tips for doing the looks I love best, at home.

BUT . . . before we get to the fun part, I need to insert a serious disclaimer about beauty. It's only skin-deep, right? Well, make sure you're taking care of your skin – even if your skin is too young to show signs of aging. As you probably know, I grew up in Orange County, where sunbathing is about as ingrained as teeth brushing. I basically lived on the beach, and when I wasn't on the beach, I was playing soccer or tennis outdoors. Unfortunately, I was never as diligent about sunscreen application as I should have been. I didn't burn very often so I didn't think that I needed to wear SPF everyday. You can imagine my surprise when the dermatologist told me – at the ripe old age of fourteen – that he would be removing precancerous cells from areas on my back. Even after visiting a plastic surgeon post-surgery, I still have the scars today. So slather up, even if it's not particularly 'sunny' outside, or you think your skin tans so easily that you never burn. Those UV rays are a serious threat to your health, and I bear the battle wounds to prove it!

DAYTIME LOOK

'The goal here is to create a look that is pretty and effortless –
direct sunlight has a way of revealing make-up, so keep it light and low-key!' – Amy Nadine

FACE

After you've washed, toned, and applied day cream to your face (with SPF!), follow these steps:

1. Warm up a dab of sheer foundation or tinted moisturizer in the palm of your hand, just enough that it's undetectable. (Don't stress about blemishes. Those will be addressed later.)

2. Do a quick sweep all over your face *and* neck with a foundation brush or, believe it or not, your fingers. (Fingertips are the best means for conquering hard-to-reach areas, just be sure to wash them first.) If you protect your face with sunblock and a hat, your shoulders and face

may not be the same colour. Match the foundation to your chest, or else your face will be dramatically paler than your body (which for anyone in my line of work can be a red-carpet *disaster*).

3. Dab concealer on any problem areas and blend it in. Using a concealer that's an exact match in colour can correct problems like under-eye circles, blemishes, or broken capillaries (see p. 138 if you have more questions about this).

4. Dust some translucent loose powder along the forehead, nose, and chin, leaving cheeks untouched.

BLUSH AND BRONZING

While lots of blush colours work well on most people, one that is apricot or peachy coloured is a good, basic standby – and if there's a range, go for one that's slightly more orange in shade. Otherwise, it will turn pink once it's on the face. Cream blush is pretty, but it's high-maintenance, since it absorbs into the skin and requires re-application. So choose a matte, powder blush for day. Smile at yourself in the mirror, and sweep some onto the apples of your cheeks to create a pretty, 'flushed' effect. Then dust some translucent powder over it to set it in place.

For the California Girl glow, bronzing is key. Buy a matte, non-orange bronzing powder (it should look light brown or dark taupe) and a kabuki-style brush, which is key for mimicking a natural tan. Then follow these simple steps:

1. While looking in the mirror, suck in your cheeks.

2. Sweep the bronzer across the hollows of your cheeks and directly below and on top of your cheekbones, starting on the outside of your apples and following the bone all the way to your ears.

3. Dab some bronzer on your temples, hairline, along the sides of your nose, and under your jawline in light, circular motions.

4. Brush your neck with bronzer, too, so there's not a line between neck and face.

5. To make it 'real' looking, blend it well by using the same brush with a tiny bit of translucent powder on it – swirl it back over the areas until there are no lines between the bronzed and un-bronzed skin.

EYES

'There's no love lost when it comes to Lauren and eye shadow.
But there are other ways to accentuate your eyes.' – Amy Nadine

You can create high drama by defining your eyes with black liquid liner – it has a reputation for being tricky, but it's much easier than it seems:

1. Rest your elbow on something sturdy like a bathroom counter so that you only need to move your wrist (controlling the movement of your hand is the trick to mastering liquid eyeliner).

2. Place the brush or pen at the inner corner and drag it outward, stopping at the outer edge. Less pressure yields a thinner line – you can always go back and press harder for a thicker edge, so start small!

3. Once you reach the outer corner, pause: think of your face as a clock with a vertical line from the centre of your eye to your eyebrow as 12 and a horizontal line to your ear as 3. You're gunning for 1:30. Wing the liner out a little bit for the cat-eye look, stopping where your eye crease ends (roughly the length of an eyelash).

If this sounds terrifying, practise! And take the wing out incrementally, pausing to see how far you can go before it becomes costumey. Remember, make-up is temporary, so if you mess up, wet a cotton swab with a tiny bit of make-up remover, wipe it off, and try again. This can drastically change the shape of the eyes: it will elongate them and make them appear farther apart.

Finish the look with natural, non-clumpy mascara. Use the wand in both combing and wiggling motions, horizontally and vertically. It's the best way for reaching and defining every single lash.

LIPS

For day, it's just clear lip gloss or balm. Natural and no fuss!

NIGHT-TIME LOOK

'Lauren's event look is essentially a high-drama, dressed-up version of her daytime look: thicker liquid liner, some extra lashes, and pumped-up cheek colour.' – Amy Nadine

FACE

Start with some medium coverage foundation to even out the skin tone: think of making your face a perfect and polished canvas.

1. Use a sponge or foundation brush to create an extra-velvety finish.

2. Set it with a translucent powder puff so that you can press the powder into the skin.

3. Choose a cream-based concealer that's a half shade lighter than the foundation in the under-eye area so that it acts as a highlighter.

4. Leave your upper eyelids, for now.

BLUSH AND BRONZING

Because the face is now one flat shade, and blank (a good thing!), it's important to add some definition back in.

1. Using the same colours from the daytime palette, apply blush to the cheek apples (using a heavier hand), bronzer, and a thin coat of translucent powder across the entire face.

2. Find a nude or gold, lightly shimmered highlighting powder and, using a fan-shaped brush, sweep it above the cheekbones, from the apples to the ear. This catches and reflects light beautifully. It's always best to add highlighting powder in layers (which is why the fan brush is key); keep sweeping on more until you get it right, but keep it light. (It's much easier to apply extra than to take it off and start all over.)

3. Using a small eye shadow brush, apply a nude highlighting powder under the eyebrow arch and on the brow bone. Do *not* use a white colour: it's way too obvious.

EYES

BROWS: For a more polished look, fill in the brows with a taupe-coloured pencil or shadow. Even if your eyebrows are dark brown, don't use anything deeper than taupe. (Darker colours should be exclusively for the runway or the stage.) The goal here is to fill in any holes. For better perspective, be sure to stand a foot away from the mirror when applying.

1. Start at your arch and work outward with small strokes, following the direction the hair grows all the way to the end of the brow.

2. Go back to the arch and shade inward, if necessary.

3. Keep checking the mirror to ensure that it's even.

LIDS: Practise different liquid eyeliner thicknesses on the back of your hand. (Remember, the harder you press, the thicker the line.)

1. Starting at the inner corner of your upper lash, draw a thin line about one quarter the length of your eye.

2. Then press a little bit harder until you're about three quarters of the way across.

3. Then press even harder until you're a few millimetres past your eye.

4. Finally, aim for 1:30 again and wing the liner up and outward.

You don't have to create an eyeliner swoop in one motion – keep adding more until it's perfect.

LASHES: Extra lashes go a long way toward adding volume, thickness, and length.

1. Coat your top and bottom lashes with plumping mascara (comb out any clumps if necessary).

2. Add three Shorts and six Mediums to the upper centre and outer corners (see p. 131 for more on adding lashes).

A good way to add definition is to use eye shadow to line the bottom lashes. (Since it's not being used as eye shadow here, I'm okay with it.) Though a soft black is the norm, sometimes an outfit calls for electric blue, deep purple, pewter, or copper.

1. Wet a thin, angled brush with water; then dip and swirl in the shadow until it's loaded.

2. Draw on the back of your hand first to practise and dump any clumps.

3. Starting at the outer corner of your bottom lash line, drag the brush inward with small flicks of the wrist, making it thinner as you approach the inner corner. Only apply shadow to three quarters of the length of the eye, to help create the illusion of a longer, almond-shaped eye.

For extra evening drama, you can use whichever technique you prefer to apply a black kohl pencil or eye shadow on the water line (that area between your lashes and eyeball). Either place the pencil at the centre of your eye, close your lids on it, and drag the pencil from the centre to the outside of your eye (keeping your eye shut), or gently pull your lower lid away from your eye and trace the pencil or shadow brush directly on the water line, repeating the movement on the upper lid.

Touching Up on the Sly

Back in the day, before cream blushes were invented, lipstick was the non-powder alternative. It really does deliver a great, on-the-go flush, which is the best thing to do if you need to quickly wake up your face. Rub a bit of lipstick between your fingers to warm it up and then dab it directly on the apples of your cheeks.

LIPS

Because the eyes are so dramatic, it's best to finish this look with a nude-coloured lip, creating a sultry and smouldering effect.

1. Fill in the entire natural shape with a nude-coloured pencil (this helps it last longer). You can use a pinky brown, a brown-nude, or a soft taupey nude.

2. Follow with a nude-coloured lipstick: matte, silky, or shimmery, depending on your mood.

3. Finish with a sweep of pearlized nude or clear lip gloss.

A lot of people are scared to wear nude lip gloss for fear of looking washed out. Because the eyes are so pumped up and there's plenty of cheek colour, this won't be the case here!

MASTERING FAKE EYELASHES

False eyelashes sound terrifying and complicated but putting them on is actually pretty easy once you get the hang of it – and they add instant glamour. I wanted no part of putting them on myself, until Amy convinced me I could do it, too. Though individual lashes are harder to control (they can flip on their side while the glue is setting), and they have to be placed one by one, the final effect is natural-looking and exceptionally flattering. Strip lashes work, too, but they're a bit more obvious.

At your local drugstore, pick up individual sets of Short, Medium, Long, and Mini flare lashes. If you order a combo pack online, make sure you buy an extra set of Minis. You'll also need lash glue – glues that dry clear are best. If you're comfortable with using your fingers, go for it (it gives extra control), though most make-up artists prefer to use tweezers. It's totally a matter of personal preference.

1. Apply two coats of mascara on your top and bottom lashes.

2. Place a small dollop of lash glue onto the back of the hand. Let it dry for at least a minute so it gets nice and tacky.

3. With tweezers or your fingers, pull out three Longs, four Mediums, three Shorts, and three Minis, and place them in separate rows on the back of your hand. (This is per eye.)

4. Starting with the outside corner of one eye, place two Longs on the very end, as close to each other as possible. Point them outward and at a 45-degree angle to get a cat-eye look.

5. Directly next to the two Longs, start adding lashes, moving toward the centre of your eye in this order: one Medium, one Long, three Mediums, and then three Shorts. If you don't have a lot of space between your lash line and your eyebrow and the Longs look too costumey, swap them out for Mediums (five Mediums and five Shorts).

6. On your bottom lash line place three Minis on the outside corners, carefully inserting them in between the real lashes. If your own lashes are super long, use three Shorts instead. Just make sure that you apply them so that they're pointing down and not up (invert them).

PERFECT MAKE-UP IN LESS THAN FIVE MINUTES

'Some things are good in small doses: too much make-up can sometimes make you look too "done", particularly if you're doing nothing more than running around town for the afternoon.' – Amy Nadine

Amy Nadine has trained me well. Now I can look great in six easy steps:

1. Using a sponge, apply a powder-foundation formula (a cream base that turns into a powder). It's simple to use and because it provides great coverage, you can skip the concealer and powder. You can literally 'wipe' it on your face and neck. (30 seconds)

2. Apply blush to the apples of your cheeks and bronzer to your hairline, temples, cheekbones, nose, chin, and neck. (60 seconds)

3. Line your eyes with a kohl pencil or wet eye shadow. (60 seconds)

4. Apply mascara. (60 seconds)

5. Slick on your favourite lipstick or gloss. (10 seconds)

6. With your 80 seconds to spare, either add one pretty wash of colour to your entire eyelid and crease before you apply the liner (this doesn't work for me but looks great on my friends!), fill in your brows, or quickly spot-conceal.

HOW TO GO FROM DAY TO NIGHT IN LESS THAN 10 MINUTES

You don't have to start your make-up from scratch when you're heading straight from the office to an event, or from school to a party. These key steps will transform your face:

1. Assess your make-up. If it's cakey, mist your face with a refreshing toner and smooth out any creases with a wet sponge. If the foundation is gone, re-apply a powder-foundation formula with a sponge. (60 seconds)

2. Re-apply bronzer and blush with a slightly heavier hand. Add a highlighting powder just above the cheekbones. (60 seconds)

3. Add a wash of colour to your eyelid – it can be consistent across the lid, or you can do a darker shade in the crease. If it's the latter approach, blend with your fingertip. (60 seconds)

4. Redo the eyeliner and make it thicker and/or elongated. Apply liner to the bottom lash line and on the water line. (60 seconds)

5. Put on another coat of mascara. (60 seconds)

6. Optional: add some false eyelashes. (180 seconds)

7. Slick on a nude, light pink, or peach lipstick and gloss. (60 seconds)

MAKE-UP BRUSH TIPS

You've probably thought about the best make-up for you, but don't forget to focus on the tools you need to apply it well. A good brush can be pricey but can make a real difference. And if you take good care of your brushes, they can last for a decade. But just because a brush costs a lot doesn't mean it's the best. Test it against your face – it should feel soft and luxurious, not coarse and scratchy.

Brushes have different uses and come in many shapes, sizes, and bristles. There is a rule of thumb that you use natural fibre brushes for powder products and synthetic brushes for cream products, but Amy Nadine breaks it all the time, so I do, too. For instance, you can use a natural brush to apply cream foundation if you work it in circular motions to blend for a seamless finish.

If you're the type who wants a tool for everything, you can have thirty-three precision brushes. If that's a little too specialized, you could do with just ten: synthetic brushes for foundation, contouring, concealer, and cream blush; then natural fibre brushes for powder, blush, eyebrows, eye shadow, eyeliner, and bronzing. If you're a minimalist, you could get away with owning only five: a synthetic brush for foundation and cream blush, a tapered blending eye shadow brush, a medium-full round blush brush, an angled firm brow brush (this is when you want coarse hairs), and a big round kabuki-style brush for blending and bronzing.

Once you have the brushes you need, it's important to take care of them. Wash them gently with mild soap and warm water weekly, or after each use if you have acne-prone skin, then lay them flat to dry on your counter. For natural fibre brushes, try not to get the hairs wet at the base by the metal holder or they will loosen and begin to fall out.

HOW TO CONCEAL . . .

UNDER-EYE CIRCLES

Some people are just genetically predisposed toward dark circles; others only encounter them after super-late nights. Regardless, there are quick ways to fix them.

After you're finished with eye shadow, liner, and mascara, wipe off any make-up that might have travelled before putting on under-eye concealer. However, any liner on the bottom lashes should come post-concealing.

Choose a cream-based formula that's not too watery, or else it will end up in the creases. Pick a colour that's only one shade lighter than your foundation or natural skin tone, otherwise you'll look like you have a goggle tan!

1. With a sponge or a flat synthetic-bristled concealer brush, warm up the product a little on the back of your hand before placing it in the centre of your under-eye area.

2. Using small strokes, move from the centre toward the inner corner of the eye; then retreat to the centre and head to the outer corner. Going 'against the grain' creates better coverage, sort of like shaving your legs against hair growth.

3. Immediately after, apply loose or pressed powder to 'set' the make-up. Use a sponge first, and then sweep extra away with a clean bristle brush.

BLEMISHES

Whatever you do, don't pick at acne or skin irritations, and try not to over-dry them with topical treatments. Fiddling with your face will make it much tougher to conceal the blemishes and can add days to healing time (not to mention, a majorly increased risk of scarring).

If you have a whitehead, it's totally understandable that you might want it off your face. But don't squeeze it! This, too, will make it last days longer. Instead, take a hot shower to open pores, then hold a hot wet washcloth on it for at least a minute. This should allow you to gently 'rub' off the head without inflaming it. Mist your face with toner and let your face dry. Apply foundation and see if that provides sufficient coverage. If it's still visible, find a concealer in the exact shade of the foundation. Using a concealer brush (thin, pointed ones are better than a flat under-eye style), dab a small amount on the blemish in quick, swirling motions. Blend away the edges with your finger and set with powder.

If you have a red blemish, use a green-based concealer.

SPECIAL-OCCASION LOOKS

After you've mastered a classic daytime and night-time look, you can vary it. Sometimes, a black minidress calls for something vampier on the lips, while a more romantic gown occasionally requires something softer and sparklier.

BRIGHT LIPS

If you want to replicate a '40s Hollywood glam look, skip the liner on the lower lashes and use a nude-coloured blush. Then apply a bright lipstick: red, hot pink, and fuchsia are all deeply flattering – and some girls can really pull off a dark vamp look! (For more tips on attempting a bright red lip, see p. 144.)

To make the colour last all night, apply the lipstick and then blot with a tissue. Load an eye shadow blending brush with loose powder and tap on to the entire lip area. Then layer on another coat of lipstick. To prevent feathering, dip a cotton swab in powder and carefully trace the outer rims of the lips.

METALLIC SHADOW

To make your eyes more striking, skip the black liner on the bottom lash line and use a metallic eye shadow. Antique gold is great, but pewter, steel, navy, and purple also work, so long as they're a touch metallic.

To properly finish the look, add a pearlized nude or gold shadow to the tear duct and inner corners of the bottom lash line. This will open and separate the eyes.

MASTERING THE SMOKY EYE

The key to a smoky eye is to blend, blend, blend.

LIGHTER ON THE LID, DARKER IN THE CREASE: This is the traditional smoky eye. When it first burst onto the scene, it was executed with grey tones, though it's easier to wear with warmer colours, like coppers, golds, fawns, and chocolates.

1. Apply a fawn colour all over the lid with a lay-down brush (a flat eye shadow brush) and a copper in the crease with a precision dome-shaped brush.

2. Take a big, clean, blending brush and sweep back and forth over the crease like a windscreen wiper.

3. Go back over the crease with a gold shade, concentrating on the area just above it.

4. Blend again with a clean brush.

5. Add a nude colour to the brow bone and near the tear duct.

6. For more drama, add a copper colour to the lower lash line before coating the water line with kohl liner or shadow.

7. Apply mascara.

DARKER ON THE LID, LIGHTER IN THE CREASE: This is the equally dramatic, reverse smoky eye.

1. Apply black shadow along the upper eyelash line with a lay-down eye shadow brush.

2. Using a blending brush, cover that ground again while gently working the eye shadow up toward the crease with tiny horizontal strokes.

3. Go back over the lash line another time, adding even more black shadow before slicking one coat onto the bottom lash line with a small, precision, dome-shaped brush.

4. Add a nude shimmer powder to the brow bone and tear duct.

5. For extra drama, create the 'sunset effect': add a gold or burnt sienna to the crease.

GETTING RED LIPS RIGHT

It's a powerful statement, so the key here is to keep the rest of your face simple. In fact, if you're using red lipstick to transform your face from day to night, you might want to take some of your eye or face make-up *off.*

It can be tricky to find the perfect shade, so go to a make-up counter and try as many as you can. Some women look best with a shade that has blue undertones; others need something more orangey. Be careful to stay within the shape of your actual mouth. Use a tissue to blot your mouth, apply powder, and then add another coat of lipstick to ensure that it stays.

Unless you want to look overdone, never pair a dramatic eye with a strong lip. Bright lip = light eye; dark eye = nude lip.

CHAPTER EIGHT

Hair

*J*ust like with fashion, there are major hair trends: one season every girl on the runway will sport a pixie-ish bob; during another, it's long, saltwater-kissed waves. I've done my share of hair experimenting – in high school I dyed mine maroon, red, brown, and even bleached it, and a few years ago I attempted a bob, which looked less chic and more soccer mom. But after those few minor lapses in judgement, I pretty much decided to stick with what works best for me: long, blonde hair, styled with a loose curl. I justify this with a simple argument: yes, hair grows – but it grows slooooowly!

Sure, there have been times when I've desperately wanted a different look. But wise hair stylists have pointed out to me that what I'm craving, whether it's perfect ringlets or sleek, black straight hair, is not attainable with scissors, since what I'm asking for is completely different hair. Much like with your figure, it's best to play up what you already have than try to override what nature gave you.

If you're dead set on a transformation, try it out first. You wouldn't buy a car without test-driving it, so do a little research before doing something irreversible. If you want a new hair colour, march yourself down to the closest wig store (not a cheesy Halloween store, a nice wig store) and try on as many as you can. I've saved myself from some near disasters this way. You can also use colour drops, which you apply to dry strands, to check different shades. (The colour washes out in the shower.) The drops won't lighten your hair, though. If you're gunning for length, clip in some extensions before you go to the trouble of growing it out, and if you want something shorter, pin your hair up into a faux-bob first.

I first met Christine Symonds when she was working at the Warren-Tricomi Salon in Los Angeles, and while I'd always had a pretty good handle on styling my own hair, when she got her hands on my head it was eye-opening. She was great about listening to what I wanted, which is sometimes a difficult quality to find in a stylist. When I became obsessed with goddess braids and twists, she found countless ways to incorporate them into my hair-style, ultimately turning my otherwise relatively unremarkable hair into my favourite outfit accessory of all. She also helped me get healthier locks. One of the pitfalls of maintaining longer strands is that the ends get dry: if you stop to think about it, those final inches have been on my head for a long time, and they've had many intimate moments with heat-based styling tools and other damaging factors. This is why it's become extremely important for me to learn how to take care of my hair; having it processed and styled constantly really takes a toll.

Since Christine is pretty much my hair guru, I wanted to impart her wisdom to you, too. I'm also sharing some at-home hair colour wisdom I got from another one of my hair-stylists, Kristin Ess. She knows exactly how to pinpoint that perfectly natural shade. So read on for advice on making the most of what you have.

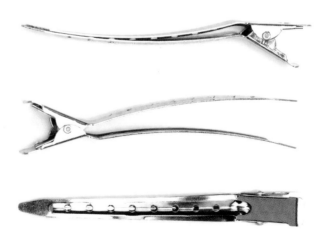

MAKING YOUR HAIR WORK FOR YOU

'No matter how well you style your hair, the most important thing is its health. Damaged hair is never going to look like the luxurious locks in a shampoo commercial.' – Christine Symonds

Besides the years of training and practice that your stylist has on you, that post-salon 'wow' factor is also due to having a set of unhindered hands – and eyes – on all parts of your head. Quite frankly, it's tough to do your own hair. But despite these limitations, you can get pretty close.

First and foremost, you have to keep your hair healthy – it's difficult to smooth and control dried-out strands and frayed ends. Invest in a good cut and quality products that are catered to your specific hair type, and splurge on a deep-conditioning treatment once a month. This adds a ton of shine! (If you don't want to go to the salon, there are hydrating hair masks you can buy at any beauty store that will do the trick at home.)

When you sit down in your stylist's chair, be realistic about the haircut you can handle. If you want to take a shower and walk out the door ten minutes later, certain styles just aren't for you.

WORKING WITH CURLY HAIR

Curly hair is fragile and prone to dryness, so make sure you're keeping it super moisturized. If it gets too brittle, it will become extra-prone to breakage. Invest in a light and hydrating conditioner.

- Ask your hairstylist to cut long layers into the curls – this will add a little volume. Just make sure the stylist doesn't go crazy, since you don't want a triangular-shaped head of hair.

- Let your hair air-dry (leave yourself plenty of time in the morning) and keep your hands away from it until it's dry to avoid creating frizz. Once 90 percent of the moisture is gone, you can style and play with it all you want.

MASTERING THE PERFECT WAVES (AND MAKING THEM LAST!)

The idea here is to make your hair look like it is naturally full of body, so don't worry if the curls aren't perfectly symmetrical.

- Apply a volumizing or texturizing mousse to freshly washed hair.

- Using a towel, roughly dry your hair – flip your head upside down and rub vigorously to create some lift at the roots.

- Once your hair is completely dry, using a 1"-1.5" curling iron (anything smaller will create ringlets), wrap medium sections of hair around the barrel away from your face. This doesn't have to be perfect – you can choose sections at random – but make sure to get all of your hair.

- Comb your fingers through the waves to break up the curls a little bit, and finish with a light-hold hair spray.

- At night, put your hair in two loose, low buns when you sleep. Twist the hair toward the centre of the head to maintain the direction of the curl.

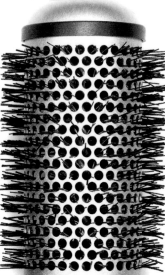

A STEP-BY-STEP GUIDE TO THE BEST AT-HOME BLOW-DRY

It can take some time to master this, so practise, practise, practise! In the interim, invest in a good flat iron to smooth out your hair afterward, if you can't get it perfectly sleek immediately.

- Divide your hair into three sections, two at the base of the neck, and one rectangular section up top: clip up the hair that you're not working on so that it stays out of the way. If you have a cowlick, attack it immediately, so that you can control it before it starts to dry. Otherwise, start at one of the sections at the base of the neck.

- Aim the blow-dryer in the same direction the hair grows to minimize frizz. Most dryers come with an attachment called a nozzle, which streamlines the hot air and directs it through a small opening at the end. This is very important to use if your hair is difficult to manage.

- Once you reach the top of your head, grab a medium-sized round brush and blow-dry the pieces back and away from the face. This creates lift at the roots – and those perfect swept-back-looking pieces around the face.

- If your hair is super fine, take four large Velcro rollers and position them in a row across the top of the head. Just make sure to wrap the hair away from your face.

- If you have a fringe, leave it for last and switch to a flat brush – you don't want any extra volume here!

SPECIAL OCCASION HAIR

It may be counter-intuitive, but don't spend too much time fiddling with your hair before a big event – less is always more. The look should be natural, soft, and *touchable* (easy on the hair spray!) so that you feel like a slightly fancier version of yourself. Overdo it and it will look more like bad prom/bridesmaid hair – or worse, a helmet.

SIMPLE UNDONE UPDO

Undone elegance at its best!

- Follow the steps above to create some waves – you want extra texture in your hair for this look to hold. There's no need to curl your entire head: focus instead on the pieces around your face and the top section of hair.

- Using the line from your forehead to the base of your neck as a guide, divide your hair into three vertical sections. Leaving the two side sections alone, gather all the hair in the middle section and pull it into a low, loose bun. Fasten it with a clear hair tie. Taking random pieces of the bun, pin them into a low, wide shape. Think of it as though you are mirroring the shape of your hairline.

- Incorporate the sides bit by bit, loosely pinning small sections into the bun.

- Let any short layers around your face fall naturally.

- Spray lightly with hair spray.

SLEEK PONYTAIL

This is a great, super-modern night-time look.

- Prep already dry, straight hair with a polish to tame any flyaways.

- Figure out your parting: one in the centre will make the look a bit bolder, but a side parting works well, too. You can also forego one altogether.

- Gather your hair in one hand and position the bundle at the occipital bone, which is where the back of your head starts to curve down.

- With your free hand, use a boar-bristle brush to smooth all the hair into the ponytail.

- Using a metal-free hair tie, secure the ponytail (the smaller the band, the better).

- Take a small strand of hair and wrap it around the elastic for a more polished look; use a hairgrip that's the same shade as your hair to fix the end down.

Hint: for a day-friendly version of this look, keep it all a bit more tousled. Instead of using a brush to smooth the hair, use your fingers to create a beachy vibe.

EXECUTING THE GODDESS BRAID

Full disclosure: the first time I wore a side braid, it was to hide an unfortunate self-fringe-cutting incident. But then I ended up loving the way it looked. If you're feeling bored with your hair, adding a braid or twist can make a simple hairstyle more interesting.

- Apply a finishing cream to hair to tame any flyaways. (Avoid serums since they can make hair look greasy.)

- Gather a one- to two-inch section of hair (depending on the thickness of the strands) and braid to the desired length.

- Secure it to your head with hairgrips that match your hair colour – I like Scunci's 'no slip grip' ones.

- Spray with a light-hold hair spray.

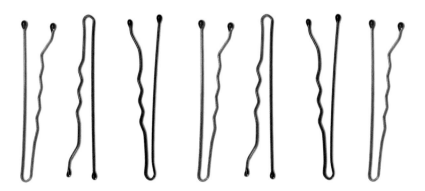

WORKING HAIR ACCESSORIES INTO YOUR LOOK

Adding vintage clips, leather cord, and even simple headbands is the perfect way to play up your hair with a minimal investment of time and effort.

HEADBANDS: This is a great go-to if you want to keep your hair out of your face, especially if you're attempting to make it last for two days in a row. Make sure that the headband sits forward on your head. It should be only an inch and a half from your hairline.

LEATHER CORD: Either a strand of suede or even fun ribbons are a great way to get a bohemian vibe (an antique necklace works, too). Tie it around your head so that it runs across your forehead. Be sure to choose something dainty: the larger the piece, the more attention it draws.

HAIR CLIPS: Search out big antique earrings or brooches at the local flea market and superglue them to barrette backs. Clip on the side of a bun for instant glamour, or leave hair down and pin up one side for a retro-inspired look.

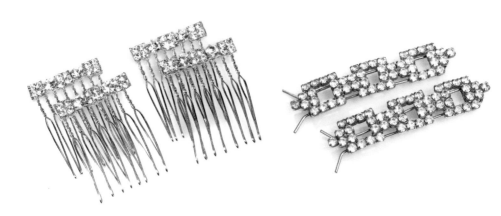

HOW TO MAKE YOUR HAIR LAST BETWEEN WASHES

Ideally, you should wash your hair every other day, though this can vary wildly depending on what kind of hair you have. Try to be consistent: your scalp will produce an appropriate amount of oil once it knows what to expect. (In fact, it will eventually self-clean if you leave your hair for long enough, though I don't recommend testing this out! It's a little gross.)

- Invest in a high-quality dry shampoo. Spray on your roots, let it sit for a few minutes, and then brush the powder through. These dry shampoos smell great and go a long way toward controlling grease.

- Keep your hands out of your hair! The more you touch, the more you're likely to stimulate your scalp. Also, there's plenty of oil and dirt on your fingertips, which you're essentially donating to your hair.

- Save the conditioner for your ends, which need the most moisturizing. Often it's too heavy on the roots anyway and will make it more difficult to style hair.

GETTING HAIR COLOUR RIGHT

'Changing your hair colour should be fun.' – *Kristin Ess*

There are lots of options when it comes to getting your hair dyed, from single process (the same shade all over, without any highlights), to lowlights (when darker pieces are added into the mix), to toner, which is essentially just a gloss. The most important thing is to find a colourist who you have complete confidence in. (It can be difficult and costly to correct bad dye jobs.) Essentially, you need your equivalent of my Kristin Ess. As mentioned, I strongly recommend going to a wig store first to rule out shades that will absolutely not work with your complexion and then trust your pro to find a good, flattering tone. Any reference materials like pictures from magazines are good to bring along so your colourist can get a clear idea of exactly what you like. (It can be better than words, since those can involve a lot of -ishes and -esques . . . you know, like a strawberry-blonde-ish auburnesque colour that's not too red!)

DYEING YOUR HAIR AT HOME

If your hair is a very basic colour, and you're not interested in the complexity of highlights and lowlights, it's safe to do a temporary colour gloss or glaze at home. This isn't a bad move, too, if you're trying to extend the time between trips to your colourist, since they can keep hair vibrant and shiny for not a lot of cash. Look for colours on the shelf that are labelled 'gloss,' 'glaze,' or 'wash out within four weeks.' These tend to be the subtlest, and thus the easiest to use – plus, they usually don't have any peroxide or ammonia so they'll eventually rinse out.

CARING FOR
COLOUR-TREATED HAIR

Every time you shampoo your hair, you're stripping a little bit of colour out of the strand – this can be helpful if you went too dark, but if you'd like to prolong the life of your treatment, try to wash your hair only every other day. Products created specifically for coloured hair are also a good investment, since they can actually add colour back into the hair.

Quick Tip:
Controlling Static

This becomes a particularly annoying problem in winter, when the air is dry and crackly. Plus, warm woolly hats and winter jackets don't help! There are a few things you can do to minimize flyaways.

• Gently rub a tumble dryer sheet over your head. It sounds crazy, but they smell great and they keep static in check.

• Spray a product like Static-Cling into all of your hats and any other pieces of clothing that cause static.

CHAPTER NINE
Work and School

There's a saying that you've probably heard: dress for the job you want, not the job you have. And it's true. Just like I would much rather show up at a cocktail party looking too fancy, rather than too casual, I believe you should take it up a notch in the workplace. It shows a certain attention to detail. If you're not a slob about your shirt, it's pretty safe to assume that you're not a slob about your work, either.

And while office-attire shopping may not be as fun as party-top shopping, and getting dressed for work may not be as inspiring as getting dressed for a night out, caring about your personal appearance shows respect for the company's culture. Plus, it's possible to dress appropriately while still showing off your personality. Whether you're a summer intern or have been working for a few years, looking polished and acting professionally is one of your best shots at making a good impression in the office. Despite my best efforts, I wasn't given much of a choice on my first day of work at *Teen Vogue*. After spending hours shopping for my perfect first-day-of-work outfit, I showed up early only to be critiqued and re-accessorized to look more *Teen Vogue*.

If you're still a student, the same gentle guidelines apply to school attire, with a significant twist. It's important to dress nicely – nothing too short, or revealing, or ratty – but this is one of the last times in your life when you more or less get to wear whatever you want. School is your chance to test-drive every look and figure out what shapes are most flattering, particularly as your body changes. You can over-accessorize; you can justify neon; you can experiment with your hair. Just as it's important to dress to company culture, the opposite is true at school: you should dress to express your unique style because this is the time when you have the freedom to define it.

WORK

THE FOOLPROOF INTERVIEW OUTFIT

The right interview attire requires a lot of thought. The basic underlying principle should be to dress as though your mother picked out your outfit, so long as your mother is one of those people who tried to swipe you with a lint brush as you were walking out the door.

You don't have to bury your entire sense of style – after all, potential employers are looking for clues about and insights into your personality – but limit the 'flair' factor to your accessories. These should be relatively simple, too.

Aim for pieces that are tailored, well fitting, and appropriate (not sloppy, not tight, and not short). Tights and a cardigan are generally good additions, too, if you want your outfit to feel more layered and covered up.

And finally, look over your outfit the night before: make sure it's rip- and stain-free, and that it doesn't need to be steamed. It's seriously uncomfortable to come to the realisation that there's a big salad dressing stain on your trousers when you're standing in the lobby!

DRESSING FOR THE JOB

Depending on what industry you're in, your work wardrobe might not be the most exciting segment of your closet. And this is okay. Focus instead on work essentials – blazers, shirts, black trousers – that fit really well. If they're perfectly tailored, you'll be much more inclined to wear them outside of the office, too. Often, because it's the least thrilling thing to spend money on, women choose ill-fitting, overly frumpy office attire. It doesn't have to be that way! Don't settle!

And despite the monochromatic palette and anti-fashion-forward silhouettes, you don't have to leave your personality at home. You just have to be subtle about it. A beautifully patterned silk scarf, a thin black patent belt, a colourful cashmere cardigan, a tasteful, yet statement-making

Cute Commuter Shoes for Working Girl Moments

I'd never support a tights-and-white-trainers fashion moment, but I'm all for easing the commute – whether it's on foot, by subway, or behind the wheel of a car – with comfortable shoes. I used to walk two miles to and from class when I attended art school in San Francisco. The fact that San Francisco is basically made up of hills and that I had to haul about ten kilos of art equipment back and forth made heels out of the question. So I began to stockpile thin ballet flats, which I could easily toss into any of my handbags. They're perfect, because they don't look out of place in the elevator, or during those first few minutes when you're getting settled at your desk before you swap out your shoes (or one block away from school, where I stopped to change mine on the pavement). Most importantly: don't toss the fabric bags that come with fancy heels – they're very handy for storing shoes during the commute. (You don't want them floating around your bag!)

necklace – all are easy ways to make an otherwise straightforward outfit a little bit more interesting.

WORK-TO-PARTY ATTIRE

I know a lot of women who store a few pairs of shoes at the office or in the trunk of their car. This is for easy swaps in case of blisters and also for when there's no time to go home before dinner or a party post-work. (A brightly coloured pair of courts can transform an entire outfit.) If I had an office job, I'd also store a small evening clutch in my desk and a handful of costume jewellery.

When an event calls for more than a minor shift in the dress code, work it into the outfit in the morning. A dress with a pair of opaque tights and Mary Janes is easy to shift from day to night. Lose the tights and sweater and add some peep-toes and a cute bag and you have a completely different look.

THINGS YOU SHOULD NEVER, EVER WEAR TO WORK

There are several parts of the body that should never see the inside of the office: your upper back, your lower back, your cleavage, and your toes. This roughly translates to no strapless tops, no halter tops, no strapless dresses, no low-cut blouses, no low-cut trousers, and no flip-flops.

SCHOOL

FASHION VICTIM VS. FASHION PIONEER

The thing that breaks my heart the most about school is the overwhelming – yet unspoken – pressure to dress like everyone else. Caving is understandable, not only because it's nice to fit in (a form of camouflage, right?) but also because nobody wants to unwittingly become the butt of some mean girl's joke thanks to a 'strange' outfit. Now, I know I don't have to live through it again with you, but all I can say is that giving in and floating downstream with that main current is the more tragic course. Real fashion victim territory! In high school my friends and I dressed so similarly, it looked like we had developed an actual uniform: same shoes, same jeans, same belt, same top. Sure, our denim washes and shirt colours may have varied, but that was as far as we strayed. If I could do it over, this would be my motto: be brave and be different. Creating your own personal style is tricky and challenging – there will be days when you'll absolutely hate what you're wearing and want to run home for a do-over, but these are necessary steps for true mastery!

WORKING WITH A SCHOOL UNIFORM

There are lots of inspired ways to modify a standard school uniform. (Not to sound like your mom or anything, but there are plenty of ways without, um, making the skirt shorter.) If the uniform includes some sort of blazer or jacket, mine the local thrift stores for unusual badges and cool pins and decorate the lapels. If the jacket is cut baggy in the arms, roll the sleeves. And check the school policy on scarves and hair accessories: a brightly patterned scarf or headband, whether silk or cotton, is a great way to add some shots of colour, and I love working vintage barrettes into any look. If the dress code is strict, you might have to get creative, but remember: you're doing it in the name of fashion.

STRETCHING YOUR ALLOWANCE:
SUPER-AFFORDABLE WARDROBE ADDITIONS

Beyond stores like Topshop and H&M, where a bulk of the costume jewellery doesn't top £10, be sure to check your city for wholesale spots that are open to the public. This is where all the trendy boutiques stock up on necklaces and bracelets. If you go straight to the source, you're likely to save at least 50 percent. And don't overlook import stores: you can snap up an armful of Indian bangles for about £7, chandelier earrings for £10, and strands of African trade beads for as little as £3.

CHAPTER TEN
Travel

I have a love/hate relationship with my suitcase. I love my suitcase when I am filling (i.e., over-stuffing) it with lovely clothing options for fun occasions: a chiffon sundress to be worn exploring the vineyards and small towns of Italy, a sheer printed cover-up for layering over a bright bikini in Cabo San Lucas, or a tailored coat and brown leather boots intended for a fantastic dinner in a chic New York City restaurant. Then, there are those times when I absolutely hate it: the last-minute work trips that consist of red-eye flights, minimal sleep, and forking over favourite beauty products at airport security because they exceed the 50ml limit (the collateral damage of attempting to travel with only hand baggage).

Dressing stylishly while on the road involves creating outfits from a small array of pieces, which is when accessorizing and styling tricks really come in handy. The idea is to bring a few key pieces to create the illusion of an entire wardrobe, and it is best if those items take up very little space. You can make the same collared shirt work with jeans and boots for day that you can then wear tucked into a pencil skirt with heels for a nice dinner at night. And it's fun to figure this all out. Just make sure the outfits work before you get on the plane! Vacation is not the ideal time to test-drive a brand-new dress.

STRATEGIC PACKING

There are lots of variables to packing for a trip – where you're going, for how long, what you're doing when you get there, how you get there – but no matter the destination or purpose, the one constant of travelling in style is packing smartly.

There are two types of extreme packers: those who bring their entire closet for a weekend getaway, and those who can assemble fourteen days' worth of outfits in Paris using only the contents of a carry-on. Everybody wants to be the master of the second scenario: not only do you get to skip the baggage claim, but it's actually much easier to get dressed when you've thought it through beforehand and pared it down to the essentials. Plus, then you get to spend the first hour of your vacation enjoying the vacation rather than unpacking. And you get to pass the rest of your time just enjoying your trip, instead of sifting through your suitcase, figuring out what to wear.

Now I'm not a total minimalist: I will always bring more than I need (insurance!). But after years of travelling I've become a decent packer, which wasn't always the case. I learned the hard way how important it is to make a list before opening up the suitcase and throwing things in. One memorable example was the time I went on a beach vacation with my family when I was eleven years old. Being the procrastinator that I am, I left packing to the last minute and ended up shoving clothes into my suitcase in a mindless frenzy. The result: an oversized baggage charge (who knew summer dresses were so heavy? . . . I only packed fifteen!) and *not one* bikini to show for it. We were in a pretty remote spot, too, and the nearest gift shop only sold leopard-print one-pieces for a different generation. I spent my vacation running along the shore in shorts and oversized T-shirts.

As much as I would like to say I've grown up and changed my ways, I arrived in Miami not too long ago only to realize I didn't pack a single pair of shoes. (Some things never change.) But while I haven't perfected the process, I have improved my packing strategy quite a bit. A few days before take-off, I jot down a quick list of activities and events (my itinerary, if you will), along with the key pieces required for each. On one long trip to Paris I actually planned my outfit for every day and photographed them. If you have the time to do this it's great because it pretty much takes all the stress out of the process.

Once I've narrowed down my options, I make sure that everything is clean (i.e., a dress for a red-carpet event, or my favourite skinny jeans for the plane) and easy to find (I once turned my entire apartment upside down the night before a flight looking for a pair of shoes that were at the cobbler's for a re-soling). After I've outlined my outfits (with as much overlap of basic items as possible), I leave it alone until the night before, at which point it only takes about fifteen minutes to get my bag together.

MAXIMIZING SUITCASE SPACE

There are a few techniques for cramming as much as humanly possible into a bag. I find that rolling my clothing works best, not only to save space but also as a means for keeping it all relatively wrinkle-free. Shoes should be separated from each other (otherwise they take up too much room), and small items like socks and underwear should always be added last (they can slot into extra pockets of air – you can even stuff some of your socks into your shoes). To keep my necklaces from getting tangled, I roll them in washcloths; you can also store them in Ziploc bags (seal the chain at the halfway point so they don't tangle).

PRE-FLIGHT CHECKLIST

After one very unfortunate trip that landed me in two feet of snow wearing only capris and flip-flops (someone actually threw me over his shoulder and carried me to the car), I learned the importance of a weather report. It seems stupidly simple, but take a minute to check the forecast in your destination city the night before you leave to make sure there aren't any surprises. Here are a few other things you should do before you take off:

- Make sure you have key things like your credit cards and your ID – you can't get on the plane without the latter!

- Drink a lot of water at least a few hours before take-off to help combat dehydration – it also helps significantly with jet lag.

- Charge your iPod and laptop, and stock up on reading material and a snack (unless you want to pay £5 for that 'ham sandwich').

- Wear shoes that are easy to slip off at security (only wear flip-flops if you're comfortable going barefoot through the metal detector).

- Make sure you have all of your cords and chargers, and anything else that's annoying, difficult, and expensive to replace on the road.

IN-FLIGHT ESSENTIALS

I've heard a lot of horror stories about on-flight blankets – and since I'm always likely to require one (aeroplanes are cold!!!), I try to bring my own. (No, I'm not the weird passenger walking through the airport with a giant pillow under one arm and a quilt under the other – I will never understand people who pack actual bedding.) The best option is a cashmere square that's big enough to serve as a blanket on the flight, and small enough to multitask as a scarf at night. (Since there's minimal sewing involved, you don't have to spend a fortune to get a decent version.) I also bring heavy-duty face cream (slather it on as the plane is taking off and it will combat the dry air for the duration of the flight) and lip moisturizer. If it's a night flight, warm socks are a must.

WHAT TO PACK
IF YOU'RE GOING TO . . .

I drew up some sample packing lists below – everyone is different, so don't feel obligated to follow them to a T, but this is what comes in handy for me.

BEACH VACATION (ONE WEEK)

Pack carefully since you'll likely be in a relatively remote location – but summery clothing takes up much less space than heavier, winter gear so feel free to throw in fun extras.

- sunscreen
- lip moisturizer
- baseball or wide-brimmed hat (for extra sun protection)
- sunglasses
- 3 swimsuits (you'll live in them, and they take up a minimal amount of space)
- 1 pair of flip-flops (rubber and washable)
- 1 pair of daytime sandals (leather or rope)
- 1 pair of embellished sandals (for evening – I like Mystique's stone-studded pairs)
- 1 pair of trainers (for exercise and travel, particularly if it's a wintertime trip and you can't wear sandals on the flight)
- 2 sarongs (great lunchtime cover-up, plus they double as scarves at night)
- 5 white, black, or grey tank tops (no explanation necessary)
- 1 cashmere cardigan (in a neutral colour, like ivory, taupe, or navy)
- 2 skirts (ideally cut from a pre-wrinkled material like crushed silk)

- 1 white oversized shirt (great cover-up once you've had too much sun, and cute when tied at the waist or tucked into a full skirt and belted)
- 1 tunic (when it's not on you at the beach, great with jeans at night)
- 1 daytime dress (ideally something that you can throw on over a bikini)
- 1 evening dress (black or neutral is best, so that you can re-accessorize it and wear it multiple nights)
- jewellery (something colourful and tropical is a good choice)
- 1–2 vintage belts (for the tunic, the dresses, and the full skirt)
- canvas carry-on tote (that can double as a beach bag during the day)
- 1 clutch for evening (if you really want to save space, use this as your wallet as well)
- 1 pair of jeans (for the flight and chilly nights)
- 1 blazer (if during the winter months, it can work as a light jacket to and from the airport, and an extra layer in the evening hours)
- underwear (and maybe a tank top with a built-in bra for those times when you get too much sun – try not to!)

WORK TRIP (THREE DAYS)

Create a capsule wardrobe by keeping everything monochromatic – and don't stress too much. If something comes up and your trip is extended, you'll likely be able to buy what you need while on the road. Chances are, you'll be in a well-supplied city.

- 1 light trench coat (khaki, navy, or black; ideally it is also waterproof, though if you hit rain, there's probably an umbrella stand nearby)
- 1 blazer (black or navy, which can also work as a light jacket)
- 1 pair of black trousers (well fitting and hemmed to work with flats)

- 2 work shirts (white always looks crispest)
- 1 pencil skirt (black, grey, or navy)
- 1 cashmere cardigan (black or navy)
- 1 pair of opaque tights (black)
- 1 pair of high heels (black)
- 1 pair of flats (black)
- 2 T-shirts
- 1 pair of comfortable walking flats (can be a trainer or something slightly fancier)
- 1 pair of jeans (for non-work dinners with friends)
- 2 scarves (to pull off the same outfit twice!)
- 1 black tote (spacious enough to serve as a carry-on)
- jewellery
- underwear

CITY VACATION (FIVE DAYS)

Pack shoes that you know are comfortable because you'll likely be on your feet all day. (The pavements of a major city are not the place to break in previously unworn flats.) And go heavier on tops than bottoms (2:1 ratio); blouses and T-shirts take up less space, and you can wear the same pair of jeans every day and nobody will know the difference.

- 2 pairs of jeans (one should be in a clean, basic wash so you can wear them out at night)
- 3 evening/party tops (which can also work during the day)
- 1 nice blouse (for daytime)
- 3 T-shirts

- 1 cardigan (cut slightly long)
- 1 blazer or cropped jacket (crisp but easy to move in)
- 1 dress (for going to dinner or out at night)
- 2 scarves (for warmth and splashes of colour)
- 2 pairs of flats (colourful and comfortable)
- 1 pair of heels (for evening)
- 1 pair of trainers (just in case)
- 1 lightweight satchel (you need to be able to carry this for hours – it may sound crazy, but consider a leather backpack as another good option)
- jewellery
- underwear

Make Room for Shopping

I travel to New York a lot for work, and time and time again I find myself with the same dilemma. I arrive with a bag stuffed to the brim and then . . . I shop. One time I actually had to buy a new suitcase in New York to get all my clothes home. So if you're headed to a shopping destination, leave extra room in your bag. Or find an American Apparel store and snap up a cheap, nylon tote.

WEEKEND GETAWAY TO SOMEWHERE WARM

Depending on where you live, you might have a favourite quick escape – mine are usually to Vegas.

- 2 party dresses (you can't wear the same thing twice)
- 1 pair of going-out shoes (these should be comfortable, since your nights will likely be long – and involve dancing!)
- 1 swimsuit
- 1 sundress (to wear during the days – it should be a basic colour, like black or white, so you can camouflage it with different accessories)
- 1 big hat (optional – these can be a pain to travel with)
- 1 pair of sunglasses
- 1 pair of flip-flops
- 1 cotton scarf
- 2 necklaces
- 1 pair of flats (for your abused feet the day after a big night)
- 1 pair of jeans
- 2 cute tops
- 1 pair of pyjamas (for sleeping in until noon and ordering room service in comfort!)
- underwear (Spanx are optional, but a good idea if you're wearing a dress that's body-conscious)

WEEKEND GETAWAY TO SOMEWHERE COLD

- 1 pair of boots (warm and winterproof – it's best if they're not too precious since you'll be exposing them to snow and salt)
- 1 pair of jeans
- 2 T-shirts
- 1 thermal top (to layer underneath T-shirts)
- 1 pair of comfortable, stretchy athletic trousers (for putting on after any cold-weather activities)
- 2 blouses
- 1 cashmere sweater (for extra warmth)
- 1 body warmer
- 1 winter coat
- 1 woolly hat
- 1 scarf
- 1 pair of gloves
- underwear (including warm socks and long underwear)

CHAPTER ELEVEN

Events and Parties

I spend many evenings getting ready for events, whether it's a red-carpet premiere, a fashion show, or a friend's birthday party. And I have to say that it never gets old. From a clothing perspective, there's nothing that comes close to matching the thrill of putting together a special-occasion outfit.

If you're reading this book, then you're probably inclined to agree that the process of getting ready is half the fun of going out.

When I'm choosing an outfit to wear for something important, I keep three questions in mind.

1. *Is it comfortable?* There's nothing worse than spending all evening fidgeting with an ill-fitting strapless dress or tugging down a skirt that's a touch too short.

2. *Is it fun?* There aren't enough occasions in life to justify wearing something boring!

3. *Is it flattering?* You want to spend the night enjoying yourself, not wondering if your upper arms aren't toned enough for something sleeveless.

FOOLPROOF SPECIAL-EVENT OUTFITS

Special occasions are the perfect opportunity to wear a vintage gown. It can be a lot cheaper than springing for something floor length from a big-name designer, and you'll never be caught in the same dress as someone else (for more on this, see p. 47). Plus, a lot of new formal dresses tend to look like bridesmaid dresses. (Gasp! The horror!)

These days, I'll look for any excuse to don a floor-length gown (Emmys, premieres, charity events . . .), though this wasn't always the case. When I look back at my prom pictures, I'm always so disappointed that I chose such boring and traditional dresses (most of which were simple cuts and didn't extend beyond my knees). I should have had WAY more fun with it. (Trust me, after you graduate, opportunities are few and far between.)

Granted, if you're at a wedding, you don't want to attract too much attention. (That said, the bride will ALWAYS out-dress you, so don't stress too much about pulling the focus away from her.) But the only faux pas is to wear something big and white. Purists always encourage you to skip black, too, though I don't think it's too gloomy, especially if you pair it with bright accessories. When in doubt go with pale neutrals or pastels.

And while I'm not a dancer, it's definitely worth considering how well the dress moves if you are; choose something fun and full-skirted. Comfortable shoes are also a big no-brainer, because evening events tend to be long. Pick some heels with staying power that are immune to grass stains or simply accept the fact that you are going to be the barefoot girl at the wedding.

COCKTAIL PARTY: This is a chance to pick a dress that shows off your best qualities. Try something colourful and flirty.

WEDDING: I like to wear vintage to weddings, like this pale sequined dress.

PROM: It's prom! Have fun with it. If I could do it over again I'd either wear something floor-length or something completely adventurous.

DECODING THE INVITATION

I've received a lot of invitations over the years, complete with head-scratching dress codes. Smart casual? What does that even mean? This sort of unclear directive can be frustrating, since I think you owe it to your guests to take some of the guesswork out of it! Regardless, the best rule of thumb is: when in doubt, shoot for being overdressed.

Here are some general guidelines:

CASUAL: Anything goes. (Almost . . . try to put in a little effort.)

SMART OR BUSINESS CASUAL: Skirt or nice trousers, with a proper blouse or top. (Some say that you can wear jeans to a 'smart casual' event, so long as the other elements are slightly more dressed up, but I would play it safe and skip them altogether.)

COCKTAIL: A dress, plain and simple. It can be knee-length.

BLACK-TIE OPTIONAL: This is more of a distinction for guys than for girls. (It's the difference between a suit and a tux.) If it's black-tie optional, you can wear a fancy dress of any length.

BLACK-TIE: People say that black-tie always means floor length, but I disagree. So long as you're wearing something polished – with beautiful accessories – you can pull off a cocktail-length dress. It should feel distinctly evening-worthy (i.e., you would never wear it to a daytime event) to make the cut.

HOW TO MAKE YOUR OUTFIT YOUR OWN

Regardless of what dress I end up choosing for an event, I always like to add a little bit of customization to anything formal, just because I hate to feel like the dress is wearing me, rather than the other way around. Remember: don't treat your clothing like it's too precious to modify! It's the little tweaks that make an outfit exceptional – and that underline that you have great personal style! Don't go overboard, though – sometimes having good fashion sense means knowing when to say when.

BIG BELTS: If you're dealing with a dress that has a lot of fabric and volume (like something made from chiffon), a big belt can rein it all in and give you an hourglass shape. Besides adding a waistline, it's also a great way to break up a field of colour or a pattern.

LACE SLIP: A little edge of lace peeking out from the bottom of a hemline is a pretty detail. Alternately, it's a great layer to add if you're wearing something that's a bit low-cut *and* drapey. A slip doesn't really work if the item it is layered under is skintight; if that's the case, it can look trampy rather than feminine and delicate.

SOMETHING MODERN: I like to add more of-the-moment tops or accessories to formal dresses, so I'll wear a shrunken blazer or leather jacket or carry a faux-snakeskin clutch. It updates the entire look, and makes it a bit different than standard fare. You can get the same effect with a bright lip colour, fun nail polish, or a cool cocktail ring.

ANTIQUE SHOE CLIPS: Back in the day, women used to add intricate rhinestone or paste clips to their shoes. (It's a useful trick for transforming a pair of plain black courts into something evening-worthy.) These clips have a ton of uses, though: you can attach them to the straps of a black cocktail dress or add them to a basic belt. And they're readily available on eBay. Feeling a bit tougher? I once wore a pair of black stilettos that my stylist customized by affixing large spikes down the back. Don't be afraid of a good DIY project!

PICTURE PERFECT

You might not have to be prepared for red-carpet paparazzi brigades like I do, but if you're going to an event, there's a good chance you'll be in a picture or two. Follow these tips and you'll never have to banish a bad photo of yourself again.

HOW TO DO YOUR MAKE-UP FOR PHOTOS

Amy Nadine's tips for avoiding that zombie-ish effect in photos:

- Steer clear of foundation or powder that's too pale, since flash photography will wash you out. Warm up your skin tone with an exact shade, or even one shade darker – and don't forget to add bronze and blush.

- Don't use anything on the lips that's excessively glossy – it will reflect way too much light.

- Skip translucent powder, since the flash will pick it up, creating the illusion that you're wearing a veil! Choose a yellow-based powder instead.

- Before you walk out of the house, take a quick photo of your face from a few different angles – this is the best way to double-check that your face and body are a matching shade and that you don't have any unsightly make-up lines.

HOW TO POSE FOR A PHOTO

Remember, photographs lie big-time: ever hear that saying that the camera adds ten pounds? It's true. And ever encountered those people who look gorgeous in photos, but unremarkable in real life? Some people's features play particularly well to the camera (thus the terms tele- and photogenic). It's all an interaction of light and shadow – so don't take it personally if you hate every picture of yourself. It's not a very good reflection of what you actually look like. That said, there are a few things to keep in mind to look your best in photographs.

- Practise, practise, practise. In the privacy of your own bedroom, figure out your best side (we all have one . . . mine is my right side), and the smile that looks the best (relaxed but not eye-scrunching – you'll want to smile with your eyes, too). Keep in mind that what may feel insane and forced in real life might be your best photo expression. Go with it until it comes easily.

- Remember that best side? Angle it slightly toward the camera, tuck your chin out and down, and then turn your eyes toward the lens and smile. If you feel like your jaw is seizing up, try pushing your tongue against your top teeth – this engages the muscles, which actually helps relax the mouth.

- Show the loveliest angle of every body part – if it's the top of your arm, point that toward the camera.

- Never stand straight-on: turn your body a tiny bit to minimize your shape, and rest the majority of your weight on your back leg, letting your front leg fall and bend toward the camera. And stand up straight, since good posture is very flattering!

- Lift your arms ever so slightly away from your sides to engage the muscle – you want to show some differentiation between your arm and your side, too, so that it doesn't look like one big mass.

- If you're in a group shot and you're the tallest or largest, try to be in the middle, or at least in a position where you're flanked by two people – those on the end get the bum rap and will always appear bigger than they actually are.

- Study celebrity photographs – it's our job to know how to hold ourselves to show our best selves. (And honestly, after five years of being on camera, it's instinctual for me at this point.) You can pick up tons of pointers just by mimicking a pose that looks relaxed and happy. Here are a few of me to get you started:

THINGS TO AVOID WHEN
YOU'RE GETTING YOUR PICTURE TAKEN

Clothing with small patterns make video cameras go nuts (the screen will literally shimmer, and not in a good way) – plus, it tends to make the body look bigger. Bright colours photograph well and help mitigate the fact that the flash will wash you out. White is really tough – not only does it often end up looking transparent thanks to backlighting and flash, but it reflects a ton of light, which just makes you look bigger. (Darker colours have the opposite effect, since they absorb the light.) If you're being photographed from the waist up, don't wear too much volume up top (you don't have the benefit of whatever you're wearing below to balance out the outfit), and skip anything strapless, since it will make you look naked.

WHAT REALLY HAPPENS AT PHOTO SHOOTS –
PLUS, WHAT HAPPENS AFTER!

One last thing about pictures . . . It's great to take tips from pictures you see in magazines – I'm always using them for styling and make-up ideas. But please keep in mind that these are highly processed shots!

Remember what I said about people whose features are naturally photogenic? It pretty much has nothing to do with how beautiful they may or may not be in real life. In fact, this is why it's still essential to do screen tests in Hollywood – as gorgeous as someone may be, you just can't tell whose face will read well on film.

So, beyond the physical structure already at play, when you have your picture taken for a magazine, there's a veritable crew of people on-set to make sure that you look amazing: make-up artists, hairstylists, manicurists, tailors, stylists, plus a crew of assistants who are steaming and pressing every article of clothing (and there are hundreds – an entire closet's worth!). Most importantly, there's always a great photographer, too, who knows how to coax beautiful shots out of even the most unlikely of subjects. (They can make a can of

Cautionary Tale

Granted, it takes a lot of flashbulbs to turn a dress transparent, but if there's any doubt, choose a dress that's lined. I once went out for the evening with a friend only to find ourselves encircled by paparazzi when we were trying to enter the bar. We didn't give it much thought until photos came out the next morning revealing that the cameras could see right through my friend's black jersey dress. To make matters worse she had opted to go braless and had only Finding Nemo Band-Aids covering her, ahem, lady parts. Oops!

cat food look glamorous.) And this photographer has a team of assistants who are setting up and tinkering with about twenty different lights, all with the end goal of making you look as flawless and perfect as possible.Preparing sets and lighting alone takes hours.

After the shoot has wrapped, the photographer will go through the hundreds and sometimes thousands of pictures snapped over the course of the day and send an edit of the best shots to the photo editor. He or she will then go through every single image with a loup (one of those magnifying eyepieces) until they find the most flawless choice. At this point, it goes to a photo retoucher, where they remove all of the unsightlies: bumps, blemishes and stray hairs. Some magazines will even whittle arms and legs down a size or two and add some contour definition to muscles! There's an ongoing – and raging – debate about when to say when with the photo retouching.

Regardless, the image that ships to the newsstands is *sort of* what the person looks like – with a ton of help! Please keep this in mind when you're setting entirely unrealistic expectations for what you should look like. Celebrities and models have bad hair days, bad skin days and bad body days, too. But their image is so controlled, you're never going to get to see it on a magazine cover (weeklies excluded).

ENDNOTE

I know a girl who lives in New York, who, for the longest time, had only a bed and a dresser in her apartment so that she could spend her extra money on clothing. I see the point in that: I would happily live in an empty apartment if I could fill it with shoes!

But as devoted as I may be to my wardrobe, it's important to acknowledge that true style extends beyond what you look like when you walk out the door. You don't have to express this through grand gestures, either. It's the small gestures that will really set you apart, like being gracious to waitstaff and cab drivers, holding open a door for someone who needs help, or bringing a friend flowers on her birthday.

And most importantly, it's in giving thanks. Whether it's for dinner, an informational interview, a gift, a college recommendation, or even just for being a good friend, if you're ever in doubt as to whether a thank-you note is required, write one anyway. It costs nearly nothing – save for a card and a stamp – and it's so rare that it automatically wins you major points in the class category. Plus, it *feels* good, both to write and receive one.

So to that end . . .

L

Dear friends,

Style is such a big part of my life, and I am so happy I had the opportunity to share my love for it with you. Thank you for reading my book. I hope you enjoyed it... and that you learned a few things along the way!

Best wishes,

Lauren

ACKNOWLEDGEMENTS

A lot of people were involved in the making of this book, but special thanks go to:

Matt Jones, Adam Fedderly, and Tyler Jennings for working so hard to create such lovely photos, for always giving us a pink sweater to look forward to, and for listening to Disney music for two days straight.

Tara Swennen, Jennifer Teller, and Caley Lawson for going above and beyond in the styling of this book. The amount of work you put into your search for all the necessary clothing is unbelievable. We couldn't have done it without you.

Amy Nadine Rosenberg for not just making me feel beautiful, but for Disney sing-a-longs, trying weird vegetables, and getting me to take burlesque classes. I'm so lucky to be able to work with someone who is not only talented but is a dear friend.

Kristin Ess and Caitlin Rylander for working so hard to create so many fabulous 'dos and for always supplying us with a new catchphrase – 'I love this story.' Also for not only doing my hair but anyone else's who is within arm's reach. We end our days with the loveliest of crews.

Howard Huang and Jamie Huang for taking the time to photograph so many things and doing a beautiful job on all of them.

Elise Loehnen for making this such an enjoyable experience. It was so much fun to create this book with someone who shares my love for style.

Everyone at HarperCollins, especially Zareen Jaffery, Melinda Weigel, Cristina Gilbert, Erin Gallagher, Tom Forget, Barbara Fitzsimmons, and Elise Howard.

Melissa Bruno, who makes everything that can be exhausting about a book tour completely fun.

Farrin Jacobs and Sasha Illingworth – after two weeks of editing done in a Hyatt meeting room during a children's talent search, there are few people I would still like. But after many British clubs, multiple servings of questionable lunch meat, malfunctioning lights, crowds of maroon-clothed football fans, and more than a thousand photo kills, I'm still quite fond of you both. Go Crimson Tide!! (Hyatt, thanks for introducing me to the British club sandwich. It's pretty great!)

Matthew Elblonk for guiding me through the publishing process and taking care of the business stuff . . . or whatever. Thanks, buddy.

The wonderful team that makes it all possible: Max Stubblefield, Nicole Perez-Krueger, Teal Cannaday, and Kristin Puttkamer. To be honest, I'm running out of ways to thank you all. It's probably because you're pretty amazing at what you do. So thanks, again.

Credits

ALL PHOTOGRAPHS OF
LAUREN CONRAD
Matt Jones
(except pages 2 and 211)

ALL CLOTHING AND
PRODUCT PHOTOGRAPHS
Howard Huang
(except page 41)

FASHION STYLIST
Tara Swennen

MAKE-UP
Amy Nadine Rosenberg

HAIR
Kristin Ess

ART DIRECTOR
Sasha Illingworth

Fashion Credits

On the cover and pages viii and x
Dress by Alexander Berardi; Earrings
by Deszo for Roseark; Shoes by Aldo

CHAPTER 1
Page 4
Blazer by Elizabeth and James;
T-shirt by Born Famous; Jeans by Hudson;
Rings by Anita Ko; Bracelet by Borgioni

Page 7
Little black dress by Express;
Necklace by Jennifer Meyer

Page 8
Jeans by Seven For All Mankind; Collared
shirt by Theory; Necklace by Jennifer Meyer

Page 9
Skirt by Robin; Boots by Christian Louboutin

Page 10
Black top by Vince; Black heels by Christian
Louboutin

Page 11
Blazer by Lauren Conrad for Kohl's;
Coat by French Connection

Page 13
T-shirt by Riller and Fount;
Skirt by Dolce and Gabbana;
Necklace by Swarovski for Aldo

Page 14
Dress by Stella McCartney; Shoes by Christian
Louboutin; Pearls by Erickson Beamon

Page 15
Polka-dot top by Geren Ford; Jeans by Levi's;
Shoes by Yves Saint Laurent;
Maxi dress by Cynthia Vincent;
Shoes by Prada; Bracelet by Le Vian;
Necklace by Danielle Stevens; Sweater by
Neal Sperling; Jeans by Levi's; Boots by Chloé;
Necklace by Shari Wacks

Page 16
Shoes by Christian Louboutin; Miniskirt by
twenty8twelve; Blazer by Juicy

CHAPTER 2
Page 18
T-shirt by Riller and Fount; Jeans by Ever;
Necklace by Sara Weinstock

Page 22
Skinny jeans by J Brand

Page 27
Skinny jeans by Seven For All Mankind

Page 28
Straight-leg jeans by Seven For All Mankind

Page 30
Bootcut jeans by Seven For All Mankind

Page 31
Boyfriend jeans by Current/Elliott

Page 32
Flare jeans by Seven For All Mankind

Page 34
*Blue tee by IRO; White tank by Enza Costa;
Jeans by Hudson; Necklace by Sara Weinstock;
Bracelets by Anita Ko at Arcade by Rochelle Gores*

CHAPTER 3
Page 38
*Dress by Corey Lynn Calter;
Belt by Linea Pelle; Gold bangle by Le Vian*

Page 44
Left
Jacket by 1020 by Nicole

Right
Jacket by Lauren Conrad for Kohl's

Page 48
*Dress by Giorgio courtesy of The Way We
Wore; Belt by Yves Saint Laurent courtesy of
Decades; Vintage bag by Chanel; Peep-toe
shoes by Christian Louboutin;
Bracelet by Talisman Unlimited for Roseark;
Necklace by Sara Weinstock*

Page 49
*Dress by unknown (vintage);
Pearls by Erickson Beamon*

Page 51
Blue velvet dress by unknown (vintage)

Page 54
*Cobalt ruffle bikini by Rachel Pally;
Multicolour crochet string bikini by Missoni*

CHAPTER 4
Page 58
*Blouse by Phillip Lim; Jeans by Seven For All
Mankind; Bracelets by Anita Ko at Arcade by
Rochelle Gores; Ring by Jennifer Meyer*

CHAPTER 5
Page 68
Vintage necklaces courtesy of The Way We

Wore and House of Lavande

Page 70
Shoes (from left to right) by Courtney
Crawford, Courtney Crawford, Rock &
Republic, and Christian Louboutin

Page 72
Plain flat by Steve Madden; Dressy flat
by Chanel; Maroon court by Sergio Rossi;
Black court by Christian Louboutin

Page 73
Champagne peep-toe by Jimmy Choo;
Rose-coloured peep-toe by Brian Atwood;
Black satin court with diamond jewelled toe
by Giuseppe Zanotti; Cobalt heel with studs by
Rock & Republic

Page 74
Gladiator by Topshop; Gladiator (with chain)
by Givenchy; Riding boots by Chloé;
Suede boots by Christian Louboutin

Page 76
Bag by Balenciaga

Page 78
Everyday bag by Chanel; Vintage clutch by
unknown; Clutch by Sergio Rossi

Page 79
Evening bag by Chanel; Evening clutch by
Treesje; Oversized clutch by Rebecca Minkoff;
Clutch by Marc by Marc Jacobs

Page 80
Hobo bag by Rebecca Minkoff; Fringed hobo
bag by Jimmy Choo; Travel bag by Chloé;
Travel tote by Balenciaga

Page 81
Love bangle by unknown; Assorted bangles by
Sara Weinstock

Page 82
Necklaces by House of Lavande and unknown

Page 83
Studs by 14 Karats; Arrows by Jennifer Meyer;
Earrings by unknown; Earrings by Carla
Amorim

Page 84
Gold leaf necklace by Sara Weinstock; Gold
branch necklace by Sara Weinstock; Gold
locket by Lenora; Chain bracelet by Jennifer
Meyer; Multicolour stone bracelet by Borgioni;
Diamond cuff by House of Lavande

Page 86
Gloves by unknown

Page 87
Black tee by Vince; Scarf by Tolani; Jean leggings by Hudson; Boots by Chloé

Page 88
Polka-dot scarf by unknown (vintage); Black tee by Vince; Jean leggings by Hudson; Boots by Chloé

Page 89
Bag by Kotur; Scarf by Hermès

CHAPTER 6
Page 92
T-shirt by Enza Costa; Skirt by unknown; Shoes by Sergio Rossi; Bracelet by Anita Ko at Arcade by Rochelle Gores; Necklace by Danielle Stevens

Page 95
Blazer by Elizabeth and James; Silk tank by Joie; Skirt by Herve Leger; Shoes by Givenchy; Necklace by Anita Ko; Bracelet by Anita Ko

Page 96
Dress by Cynthia Rowley; Bracelet by Talisman Unlimited for Roseark; Shoes by Christian Louboutin

Page 98
Little black dress by Herve Leger
Left
Jean jacket by Seven For All Mankind; Necklace by Jennifer Meyer; Necklace

by Lenora; Shoes by Miu Miu
Right
Shoes by Giuseppe Zanotti; Bracelets by House of Lavande; Clutch by Sergio Rossi

Page 99
Left
Cardigan by Catherine Malandrino; Shoes by Dolce Vita; Pearls by unknown (vintage)
Centre
Cardigan by Lauren Moffatt; Shoes by Chanel; Necklace by Jennifer Meyer
Right
Leather jacket by Lauren Conrad for Kohl's; Shoes by Topshop

Page 100
Tank by I ♥ Ronson; Belt by Melamed; Skirt by Plastic Island

Page 101
Shirt by Joie; Skirt by BCBG

Page 102
Blouse courtesy of The Way We Wore; Skirt by BCBG; Shoes by Christian Louboutin; Necklace by Karma at Roseark; Earrings by unknown (vintage)

Page 105
Dress by Lela Rose

Page 106
*Belts by Melamed and WCM for Neiman
Marcus*

CHAPTER 7
Pages 114, 118, 126, 132, and 145
Shirt by Tibi

CHAPTER 8
Page 148, 153, 157, 158, 161, and 162
Shirt by IRO

CHAPTER 9
Page 170
*Shirt by Rebecca Minkoff; Trousers by Elizabeth
and James; Shoes by Miu Miu; Necklace by
Karma at Roseark; Glasses by Chanel*

Page 175
Dress by Zac Posen
Left
*Cardigan by Express; Belt by Melamed; Shoes
by Dolce Vita; Earrings by unknown (vintage);
Necklace by Karma at Roseark*
Right
*Shoes by Christian Louboutin; Bag by Chanel;
Necklace by Danielle Stevens; Belt by Melamed*

Page 176
*Blazer by Elizabeth and James; Shirt by
Monrow; Skirt by Theory*

CHAPTER 10
Page 180
*Blazer by Gap; Shirt by Vince; Jean leggings by
Hudson; Boots by Chloé; Scarf by Nordstrom;
Suitcase by Rimowa*

Page 186
Shirt by Vince; Scarf by Nordstrom

Page 188
Bikini by L*Space

Page 192
Dress by unknown (vintage)

Page 194
Coat by Plastic Island

Page 195
Scarves by Juicy Couture, Love Quotes, and Tolani

CHAPTER 11
Page 198
Dress by Tibi; Shoes by Christian Louboutin

Page 201
Dress by Lela Rose; Bracelets by House of Lavande

Page 202
*Dress with belt by ADAM; Necklace by Carla
Amorim; Bangle by Anita Ko at Arcade by
Rochelle Gores; Shoes by Giuseppe Zanotti*

Page 203
Left
Dress by unknown (vintage); Shoes by Sergio Rossi; Earrings by unknown (vintage)
Right
Dress by Rafael Cennamo; Necklace by Carla Amorim; Shoes by Christian Louboutin; Clutch by unknown (vintage)

Page 204
Dress by Femme Noir; Tights by DKNY; Shoes by Yves Saint Laurent; Bracelets by House of Lavande; Clutch by unknown (vintage)

Page 206
Dress by Camilla and Marc; Belt by Melamed; Shoes by Christian Louboutin; Bracelets by Bing Bang at Roseark and Anita Ko at Arcade by Rochelle Gores; Ring by Jennifer Meyer

Page 208
Shoes by Aldo (spikes not included)

Page 212
Dress by Lela Rose; Bracelets by House of Lavande

Page 216
Jeans by Levi's; Blouse by Phillip Lim; Shoes by Miu Miu; Ring by Anita Ko; Ring by Bing Bang at Roseark; Necklace by Karma at Roseark

Photos on page 2 courtesy of Lauren Conrad; photos on page 229 courtesy of Kristian Dowling/Getty Images (Left), Angela Weiss/ Getty Images (Centre), Frank Micelotta/ Getty Images (Right)

A special thanks to all of the designers included. Every attempt has been made to correctly identify the designers of the clothing and accessories used throughout.